STITCHES ON CANVAS

STITCHES ON CANVAS

MABEL HUGGINS & CLARICE BLAKEY

B. T. Batsford Ltd.

ISBN 0 7134 5377 X

Typeset by Tek-Art Ltd, Kent
and printed in Great Britain by
R J Acford
Chichester, Sussex
for the publishers
B.T. Batsford Ltd.
4 Fitzhardinge Street
London W1H 0AH

CONTENTS

FOREWORD

by Constance Howard MBE, ARCA, ATD, FSDC

I am delighted to write a foreword to *Stitches on Canvas*. It is most encouraging to see the book in print, as I have watched the progress of the authors and their work from the beginning. Mabel Huggins and Clarice Blakey are keen embroiderers, and their fascination with using canvas came about when they began to explore the possibilities of what could be accomplished on that type of material. Using a variety of yarns and other materials not normally associated with canvas, they began to work samplers, which became something of an obsession as each one led to another idea, and yet another. The authors found that they could produce striking colour combinations with yarns and stitches, and a richness of texture with ribbons and beads worked into the canvas, sometimes with stitches over stitches, in ways that had not previously been attempted. Seeing a number of the samplers, I realized that they showed a different approach from that found in most books on canvas work, and suggested to Mabel Huggins and Clarice Blakey that they might think about using their experiments in a book. Their enthusiasm was boundless, and I feel that this comes through in the text, with its many illustrations, all described with the greatest care and obvious affection.

Anyone interested in an adventurous approach to canvas work will no doubt become obsessed, too, with the multitude of ways in which canvas stitches and others can be used with ingenuity so that, with the inclusion of an exciting range of materials, jewel-like embroidery can be produced.

I believe that embroiderers who previously have tended to scorn canvas work will want to 'have a go' on seeing this book.

Constance Howard

ACKNOWLEDGEMENTS

We wish to express our appreciation to those who have helped in the production of this book. Our thanks are especially due to Constance Howard, who encouraged us from the beginning and advised us throughout. We are grateful also to Bridget Moss whose work and ideas have made a substantial contribution. Harold Blakey's excellent photographs speak for themselves, but we also wish to thank him for the generous support he gave us in many ways.

INTRODUCTION

The approach of this book is experimental and its aim is to bring to working on canvas the freedom that has developed in other embroidery techniques. We are not concerned here with traditional canvas work, in which, for example, the canvas is completely covered to produce a hard wearing surface for chair seats or kneelers.

We use the canvas as we would any other fabric and are not confined to traditional canvas stitches or yarns. Methods of working are totally free, and we hope to encourage others to join in the excitement of discovery leading to embroidery of original quality. To this end, we have worked small samplers to explore the limitless possibilities of combining all kinds of yarns and stitches on different meshes of canvas. The mixing and free use of stitches to create a given effect adds to the richness of the embroidery and develops a creative approach in the worker. One idea inevitably leads to another, as we shall show. Ideas develop by laying on threads – single strands or bunches – beads or any other materials. Moving these about on the canvas and studying the results enables the worker to see how the arrangement will work before it is actually stitched. We suggest that all experiments are kept in a file as they will be useful when the effects obtained are studied or for future reference to yarns, stitches and colour as the work goes on (*Fig. 1*).

The chapters that follow consider each of the main ingredients of design in turn. They are, of course, interdependent, but it is simpler to study them separately to realize the full importance and impact of each.

1 MATERIALS

Making a collection of materials for experiments on canvas can be a satisfying and rewarding occupation; never before has there been such a great variety. Craft shops will supply the usual materials, such as canvas and wool, but the haberdashery and knitting departments of large stores are always worth exploring. Garden centres, ironmongers and stationers can often be useful sources of interesting materials, and it is a good idea always to be on the look out.

1 A sampler made from natural materials: raffia, hemp, natural hessian, straw, wooden cube beads and two pieces of black net, which allow the deep cream of the canvas to show through. Stitches used are: satin, french knots, detached chain, rice, double cross, cretan, wheatsheaf, cross and bullion.

You will need to build up a collection of the following

Canvas This is available in two types: single and double (*Fig. 2*). It is usually stiffened with size or paste and is made of cotton or synthetic fibres; linen canvas is no longer available. **Single** canvas is more useful than double as it is available in a wider range of meshes, from 28 threads to 2.5 cm (1 in.) (very fine) to ten threads to 2.5 cm (1 in.). It can vary in colour from lemon to yellow, beige or white. **Double** canvas is made in mesh sizes from 18 double threads to 2.5 cm (1 in.) to 4. This large size is called 'rug' or 'thrums' canvas and may not be easy to buy at a craft shop but there are specialist suppliers of both the canvas and thrums for working.

Needles You will require a needle with a blunt point and large eye, called a **tapestry** needle. The needle should pass through the mesh easily without distorting the weave, and the thread must run freely through the eye to reduce wear. Sizes vary from 24, which is only suitable for a very fine canvas (18 threads to 2.5 cm (1 in.) and above) to size 14, used with thrums. **Chenille** needles are made in the same sizes as tapestry needles, from 24 (fine) to 14 (coarse), but these have a sharp point and can be useful when superimposing stitches onto an already worked background. **Sharps** and **crewel** needles, both of which have sharp points, may be needed when you are attaching leather, felt or fabric to the canvas before working stitches using the canvas mesh.

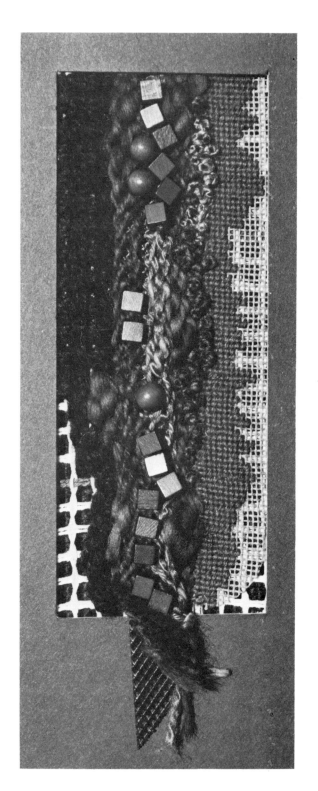

2 *Raised chain band on coarse rug canvas using Bernat Klein wools with french knots and wooden beads. Fine canvas is overlaid and stitched with tent stitch through both layers.*

Threads Traditionally, wool has been the most usual working thread for canvas because of its hard-wearing qualities and because it does not soil easily. The two types of embroidery wool are **crewel** and **tapestry**. The finest is crewel, which is available in a very large range of colours. Any number of strands can be used in the needle to give the required effect. Tapestry wool is coarser, softer and not so hard-wearing. Two or more strands can be used in the needle for work on a very coarse canvas. Because of its thickness, tapestry wool is not so versatile, and must be carefully matched to the mesh of the canvas. There is considerable variety in thickness between the different brands of tapestry wool. It is therefore often possible to select the wool of a particular supplier to match the chosen canvas. **Rug thrums** are the remnants from carpet weaving and so are very hard-wearing. The wool is two-ply and about the same thickness as double knitting wool. It has the advantage of being fairly cheap. Any other yarn can be used. The renewed popularity of knitting in recent years has provided an interesting range of yarns of many different textures and colour combinations.

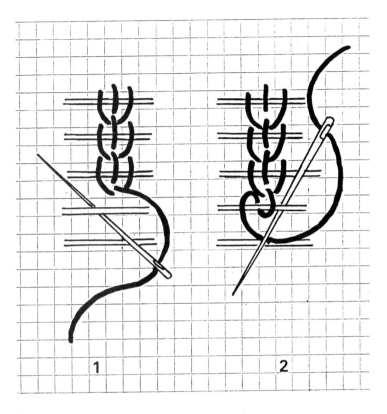

3 Raised chain band.

Stranded cotton, perlé cotton and coton à broder all provide a useful contrast to the matt finish of wool. Highly twisted threads, such as those supplied for macramé, give a totally different appearance to a worked stitch. Even household string or decorative twines sold for parcel wrapping have their uses. Raffia and raffene, although rather awkward to manage with some stitches, give a shiny eye-catching effect when used in combination with other threads.

Fabrics A collection of fabrics of various weights, colours and textures can be used in many ways. If the fabric has a contrasting warp and weft, a strip can be frayed for applying to the canvas; narrower strips can be threaded in the needle and used for working large scale stitches.

Nylon stockings These can be used in their natural colour or bleached and re-dyed. Narrow strips are cut on the diagonal and threaded into the needle. The resulting strip is rather stretchy – not unlike sewing with elastic – but gives an interesting texture, particularly if combined with wool.

Transparent materials Chiffon, organdie and net, when laid on the canvas, change the colour of the background. It is quite easy to work stitches through both layers as the mesh is easily seen. Fabric, cords or felt may be attached to the canvas and covered with transparent material.

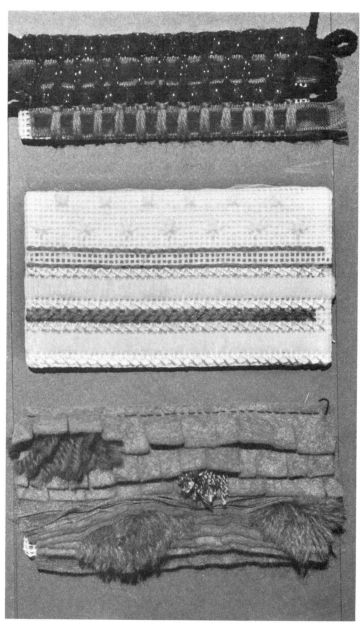

4 (Top) *Up-and-down buttonhole stitch over chenille and velvet ribbon, using a lurex knitting yarn.* (Middle) *Canvas covered with chiffon. There are two bands of straight stitches in wool underneath the chiffon, with bands of cross stitch, back stitch and long-legged cross in wool and perlé cotton, worked through both chiffon and canvas.* (Bottom) *Tightly packed strips of felt and folded chiffon are stitched to the canvas, with tufts of surrey stitch in wool and perlé cotton lying between the layers. The three top strips of felt are more widely spaced.*

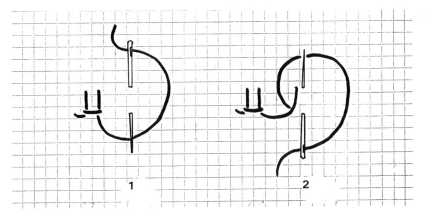

5 *Up and down buttonhole stitch.*

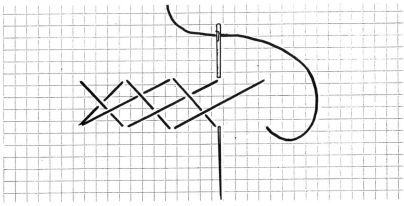

6 *Long-legged cross stitch.*

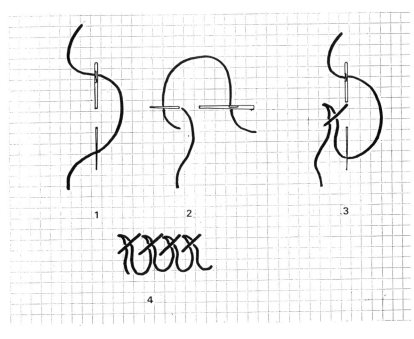

7 *Surrey stitch.*

Non-fraying materials Leather, felt or vilene, if applied to the canvas background, contrast well with a stitched area. Felt can be manipulated to give a raised texture, contrasting with flat stitchery.

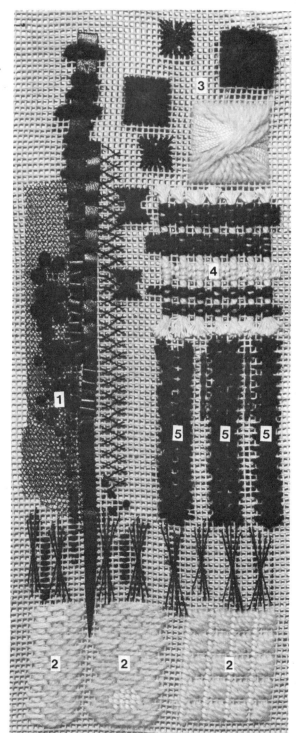

8 (1) Two strips of black shiny leather, manipulated into humps, form the centre, flanked by black net overworked with large black french knots in wool and rayon on one side and, on the other, a band of herringbone in fine black cotton, also used to work the sheaf shapes below.

(2) Underneath, three white blocks in wool and cotton, worked using horizontal and diagonal stitches to create simple fillings.

(3) Rhodes and part-rhodes stitches in perlé cotton and a variety of wools. Where thick wools have been used raised cushions are formed.

(4) Below these are short lengths of piping cord secured in bands with tent and satin stitch, using brown wool and thick white rayon.

(5) Short lengths of chain in brown lead into three columns in black wool, worked in raised-stem band and raised-chain band.

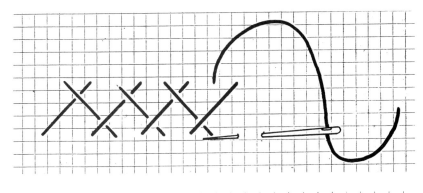

9 *Herringbone stitch.*

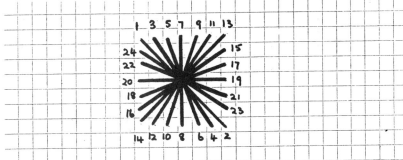

10 *Rhodes stitch.*

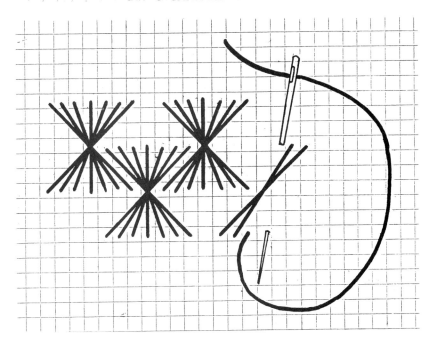

11 *Part-rhodes stitch.*

Braids and ribbons These are very useful, particularly the very narrow ribbons which can be threaded in the needle and used for working selected stitches. Velvet ribbon and braids of varying widths can be held down with stitchery. Russia and ric-rac braids can be threaded through back stitches to make an interesting texture.

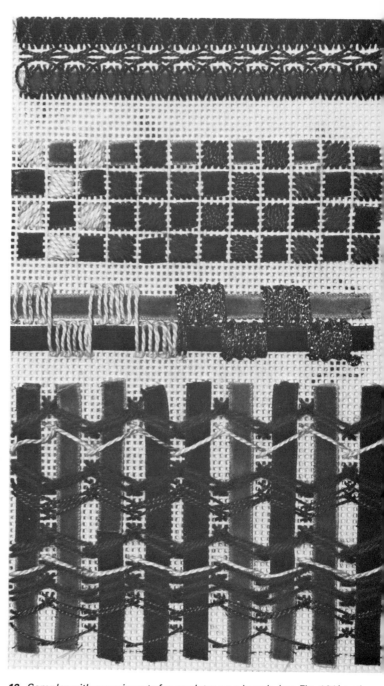

12 Sampler with experiments for use later on a bangle (see Fig. 101) and the panel, 'Spring Cabbage' (see Colour plate 12). Designed and worked by Bridget Moss.

13 An interpretation of a landscape using applied shapes in leather and suede to represent foreground masses. Velvet ribbons, groups of square stitches, chevron and tent stitches suggest a recession of planes. Couched slub cotton softens the edge where canvas and suede join. Designed and worked by Bridget Moss.

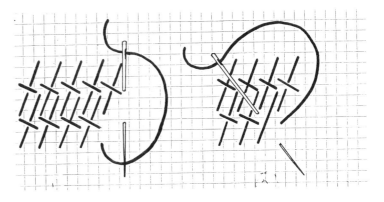

14 Tied gobelin stitch.

15 *Simple stitches and a selection of interesting materials combined to produce a richly textured sampler.*

(1) A piece of red sequin waste is secured by running stitches, straight stitches forming a chevron pattern, cross stitches in tan having the same tonal value as the sequin waste, back stitches worked with gold lurex knitting yarn, followed by a row of cross stitches and running stitches, so arranged that squares of unworked canvas form part of the pattern. The bottom edge of the sequin waste is secured by vertical stitches over one thread of canvas.

(2) A piece of blue chiffon covers the canvas with stitches worked through both layers. A length of piping cord is enclosed by the chiffon and held in place top and bottom by rows of back stitches in rust perlé cotton. Below, two strands of soft embroidery cotton are couched with gold perlé cotton, contrasting with two strands enclosed beneath the chiffon, also couched with yellow perlé cotton. The chiffon changes the colour from gold to dove grey. A band of horizontal part-rhodes stitch, worked through both layers, is followed by vertical part-rhodes stitch which holds in place a length of gold velvet ribbon lying under the chiffon.

(3) Orange russia braid crosses the width of the canvas leaving two threads between each length. Double herring-bone stitch lies under the braid and three satin stitches worked between the herringbone hold the braid in place. Where the braid is covered by chiffon the herringbone stitch is threaded and the spacing changed.

(4) Six pieces of tan leather are attached to the canvas. Chevron stitch in gold, pale tan and copper lurex is worked through canvas and leather. The white mesh of the canvas which is visible between the stitches in alternate blocks, contrasts well with the solid leather shapes.

(5) Four lengths of tangerine braid, two lengths of lurex braid and a strip of sequin waste are held in place by rows of raised chain band and long straight stitches in shades of gold, white, tan and purple perlé cotton. Both groups of stitches form diagonal lines.
Designed and worked by Bridget Moss.

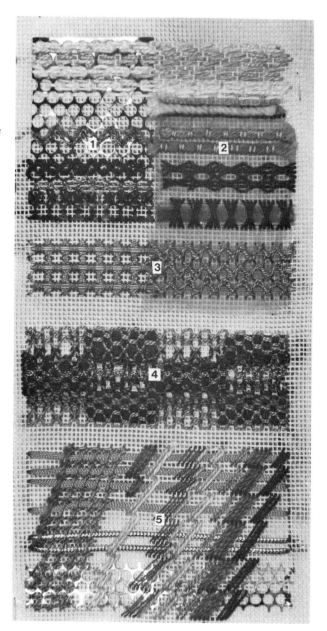

Cords Piping cord, both in its natural state and dyed, gives a raised texture if covered with close stitchery. Coloured cords need not be completely covered.

The list is endless; it is essential to have as wide a choice of materials as possible. Try using unfamiliar materials on canvas: sequin waste, shisha glass, rings, washers and beads. All of these add interesting contrasts. There may be some failures but out of these should come some really creative ideas. In addition to the collection of materials mentioned above, it will be useful to have an assortment of coloured papers. Colour photographs from magazines, gift wrapping paper, craft papers of all types will be useful in your colour experiments and as an aid to design.

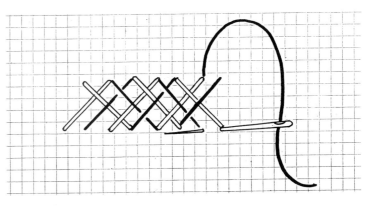

16 *Double herringbone stitch.*

17 *A pendant about 8 cm (3 in.). Shisha glass on a background of tent stitch with fishbone stitch in a darker shade worked over the tent stitch. Metallic russia braid divides the three sections and is frayed to create tassels.*

18 *Fishbone stitch.*

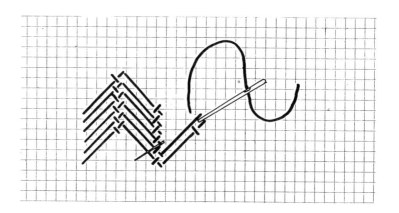

As there has never been such a bewildering choice of yarns as is available today, it will be helpful to consider some of the many ways in which they can be used. Yarns are designed for specific purposes, not necessarily for embroidery. Those which are sold as embroidery threads – stranded cotton, coton à broder, soft, perlé, crewel and tapestry wools, linen threads, silks and synthetics – are manufacturered as continuous smooth yarns in various weights. Some of these are silky, and others are matt; each kind makes its own contribution to the work. Although the yarns are smooth in quality, the results obtained on the canvas may or may not be smooth, according to the stitches used. All yarns in this category are truly versatile.

In addition to these embroidery threads, there are many others which are suitable for our purpose which have been produced for other crafts. Chief among these is the exciting range of yarns designed for knitting and crochet. These fashion yarns tend to appear and disappear with great rapidity and it is necessary to buy when you see them. As only small quantities are needed for our experiments it is a good idea to exchange some with friends. If you can work together, better still, as ideas will be sparked off more readily and there will be a shared feeling that progress is being made.

All yarns are produced from fibres, either natural, from plants (flax and cotton) and animals (sheep and camel), or synthetics and mixtures. With a little trouble it might be possible to obtain a small amount of **fleece** from a weaver or even from the hedgerows. If you are fortunate to acquire some, wash it carefully and then gently pull the fibres so

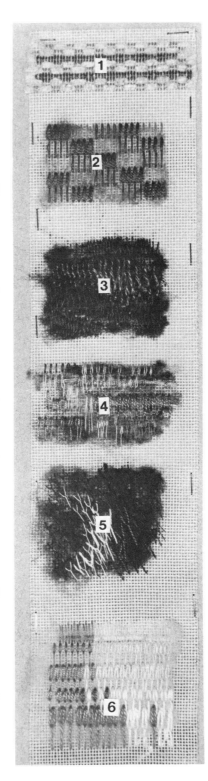

19 (1) Rayon yarn tightly couched with three stitches at intervals allowing the yarn to bulge out in between. The couching stitches are continuous and dark in tone between each pair of rows.

(2) Sheep's fleece, dyed yellow, pulled out to form a rectangular shape for the stitches. Detached chain stitches made of stranded cotton and perlé cotton in yellow and olive hold down the fleece. The stitches are in groups of four, sometimes made of single strands.

(3) The next example is worked with pale old gold on dark grey Jacob's fleece. Cretan stitches in single or double strands, perlé cotton and rayon are worked freely in varying densities and sizes.

(4) Jacob's fleece of paler grey with strips of rayon garden twine. Varying thicknesses of thread from perlé cotton to fine sewing cotton in white and gold make chain stitches, some with and some without tails.

(5) The brown patch is camel hair worked over in 'Y' stitch in a diagonal direction, using single strands, six strands of perlé cotton and coton à broder. The stitches in brown, white, grey and dark sage green are of various sizes.

(6) A more regular arrangement of **(4)**. The detached chain stitches have been worked in straight lines in a variety of yarns.

that they all lie in one direction. *Fig. 19* shows how fleece can be used in an attractive way.

Heavy wools produced for carpet manufacture are also very useful, especially in large scale work, for example to make hard-wearing floor cushions.

20 Detached chain stitch.

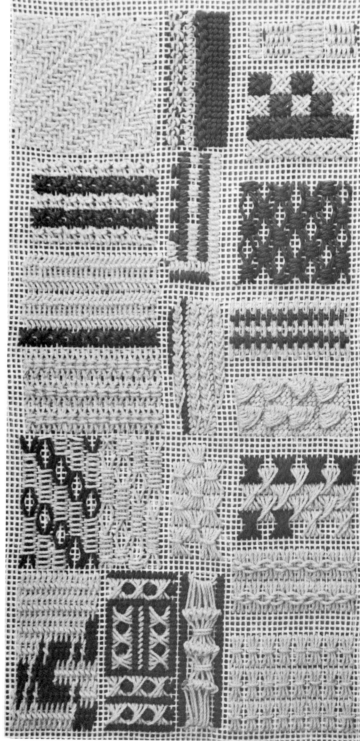

21 In macramé twine and soft embroidery cotton, the stitches include: sheaf, wheatsheaf, tent, shell, part-rhodes, arrow, spring, woven tent, raised-chain band, double-tied oblong cross, tied gobelin, chess board filling, interlaced cross and double-plaited cross.

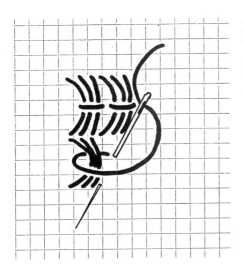

22 Arrow stitch.

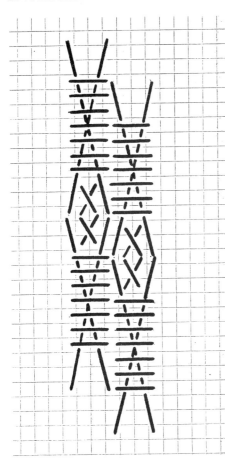

23 Spring stitch.

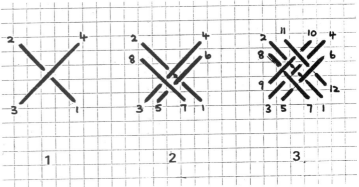

24 Woven tent stitch.

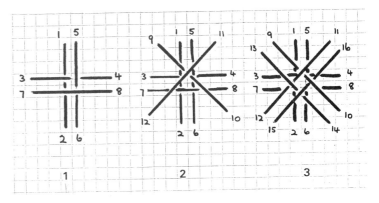

25 Interlaced cross stitch.

26 Double cross plaited stitch.

27 *(1) Rows of surrey stitch worked with narrow strips of nylon fabric in various colours contrasting with rows worked with rug wool.*

(2) Rows of surrey stitch worked with coloured raffia and strips cut from polythene shopping bags.

(3) Russia braid darned into alternate holes, to make vertical stripes. Woven with contrasting coloured ric-rac braid.

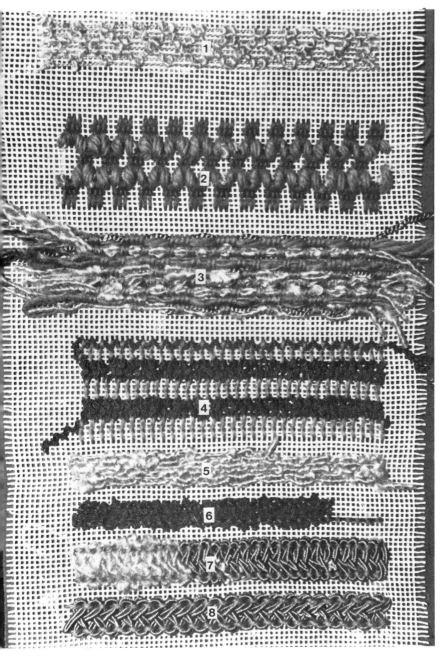

28 *(1) Underside couching worked on the wrong side of the canvas. Rayon slub is used for the couched thread with fine shiny rayon used for stitching.*

(2) Blocks of tied gobelin alternately placed in rows, the blocks linked by threading with thick embroidery yarn.

(3) A variety of yarns and cords couched with fine wool.

(4) Three rows of tied gobelin with a space of three threads between each row. Narrow ric-rac braid threaded through bottom and top loops of each row.

(5) Underside couching using a slubbed weaving yarn.

(6) Two rows of back stitch with a four thread space between, threaded with narrow ric-rac braid.

(7) Two rows of back stitch with a six thread space between, threaded with slubbed weaving yarn and russia braid.

(8) Two rows of back stitch with five threads between interlaced with russia braid.

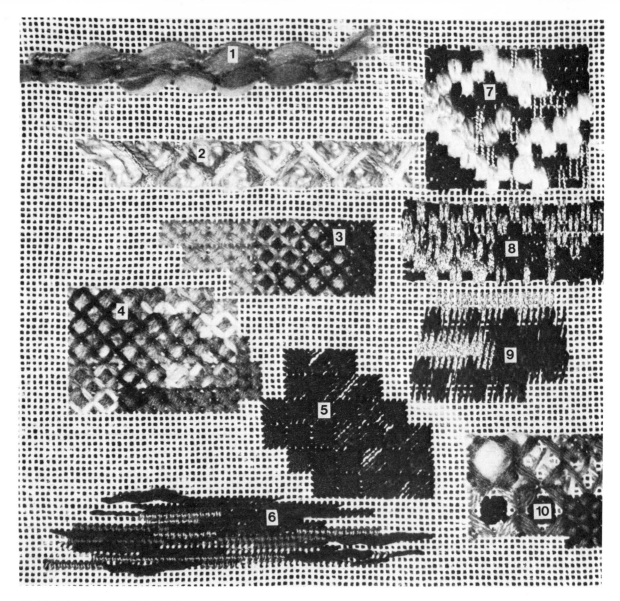

29 *(1) Slubbed Bernat Klein knitting wool, couched with wool.*

(2) Multiple herringbone stitch using four different yarns, the first row spaced, leaving eight vertical threads between each stitch. Subsequent rows fill in the spaces, leaving two threads between each.

(3) Shaded rice stitch; old gold and brown shading from all gold at one end to all brown at the other. Intermediate stitches have the cross stitch in brown and the crossing stitches in gold, then vice versa.

(4) Shaded rice stitch; variegated wool in shades of fawn and brown, crossed with gold, brown and beige.

(5) Mosaic stitch in perlé cotton, slubbed knitting yarn and shiny crochet cotton with the direction of the stitches changed.

(6) Slubbed black knitting cotton held down with tent stitch, in a variety of shiny rayon yarns.

(7) Black chenille, laid as for burden stitch, couched over two rows with two pairs of stitches in a variety of yarns: Christmas wrapping cord, perlita, heavy cream rayon and black crochet cotton.

(8) Black chenille laid as for burden stitch with pairs of stitches in gold lurex, and black and silver knitting yarn.

(9) Encroaching gobelin stitch in rows of gold lurex knitting yarn and black slubbed knitting cotton.

(10) Rice stitch showing variation in scale.

The firm, tightly twisted, smooth yarns made for macramé should not be forgotten. Using these yarns results in work of a totally different character (*Fig. 21*). Remember to save interesting strings in a polythene bag. Do not overlook garden twines. **Raffia** and **raffene** (*Fig. 27*) create a totally different effect in a design. They both readily split into finer threads and the sheen of raffene contributes a rich result suitable for jewellery, evening wear and accessories.

Continuous lengths of any yarn that will pass through canvas without damage can be used. On a coarse mesh these can include cords, braids and narrow ribbons.

Another craft which can yield interesting yarns is weaving. Unfortunately, weaving yarns are usually available only in large quantities on cops, but it may be possible to share with other enthusiasts. Smaller quantities may be available from a weaver as there are always short lengths of warp discarded when the woven piece is cut and removed from the loom. Weaving yarns are produced from a wide range of materials and include slub and other fancy yarns (*Fig. 28*).

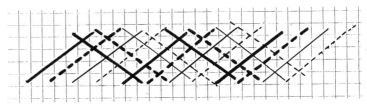

30 Multiple herringbone stitch.

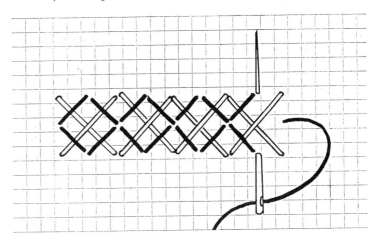

31 Rice stitch.

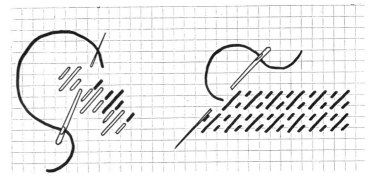

32 Mosaic stitch.

There are various forms of **slubs**; they may be softly elongated or hard and knobbly. They are introduced into the yarn during the spinning process as the result of tightly twisted fibres being followed by little or no twist. In the two-ply Bernat Klein wool slubs can be as long as 15 cm (6 in.) alternating with loose stretches up to 40 cm (16 in.).

There are many interesting and beautiful yarns that could be damaged or would not show to the best advantage if pulled through canvas. A satisfactory way of dealing with these is by laying them singly or in groups on the surface of the canvas and fastening them down with small, inconspicuous stitches. If the couching stitches are to contribute to the design, then larger stitches like detached chain may be used. Heavy slub yarns would lose their character if pulled through canvas and are also best couched. Bunches of mixed yarns and colours are attractive and could be treated similarly. Such bands could be separated from other stitches by one or two rows of tent stitch; these might not be seen but they will serve to show fancy yarns to advantage.

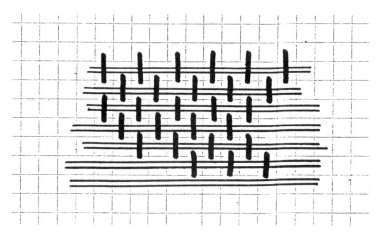

33 *Burden stitch.*

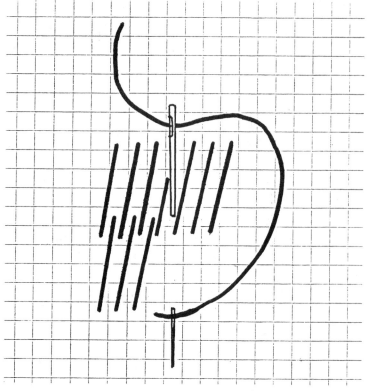

34 *Encroaching gobelin stitch.*

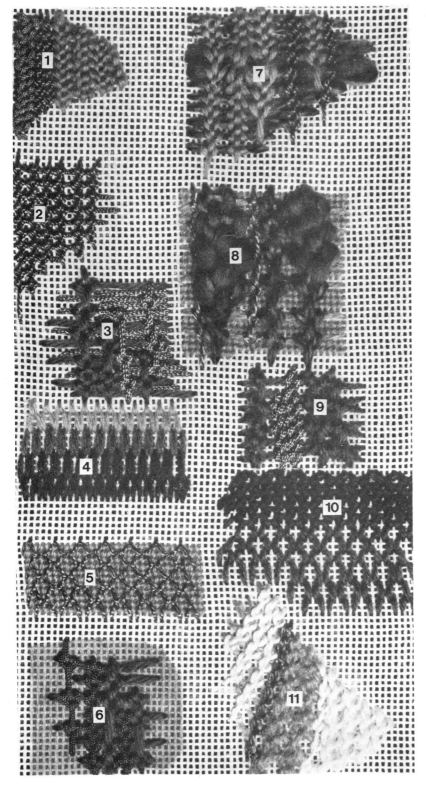

35 *(1) Closely worked raised-chain band using a rayon cord, perlé cotton and wool.*

(2) Raised chain band on a framework of rayon cord. Loops stitched with perlé cotton.

(3) Raised chain band worked over a mixture of shiny and matt bars of varying lengths. Loop stitches worked in shiny and matt threads over different numbers of bars.

(4) Wave stitch in four shades of green.

(5) Wave stitch worked over a tent stitch background.

(6) Raised chain band worked in matt and shiny threads over a blue chiffon background.

(7) Raised chain band over slubbed knitting yarn. The loops worked in a variety of yarns: wool, perlé cotton and shiny rayon.

(8) Raised-chain band over a tent stitch background, the loops worked with a variety of yarns.

(9) Similar to (3) but a more regular arrangement of stitches.

(10) Wave stitch in shades of blue and green with an increase in scale towards the bottom (from one to three threads spacing).

(11) Raised chain band worked on bars laid on the diagonal. The loops worked in a variety of yarns: perlé cotton, shiny rayon, rug wool thrums and fine wool.

36 Tent stitch overlaid with a tinsel Christmas wrapping cord to form random star shapes. Pattern darning in nylon knitting wool and bouclé wool. Eyelet holes in various sizes and threads, backed by tent stitch in perlé cotton. All worked in different shades of white.

Plate 2—

1 A group of four small beads, arranged with squares of tent and mosaic stitches using plain and multicoloured wools, to form a chequer pattern.

2 Beads in vertical rows are grouped with blocks of tent and rhodes stitches. Threads of canvas have been left unworked, both vertically and horizontally.

3 Horizontal rows of tied gobelin stitch, broken by groups of beads or by change of colour. Near the base are areas of unworked canvas.

4 Part-rhodes worked over three blocks of tent stitch with the spaces between filled with bugle beads and closed herringbone stitch.

5 Large bugle beads are placed horizontally against a multicoloured background.

6 Tiny beads secure flat discs on a background of tent and cross stitches, using an assortment of colours and yarns. Some canvas threads are left unworked.

7 Iridescent beads in vertical rows against a background of tied gobelin stitch, in an assortment of colours and yarns.

8 Rectangular beads scattered against a background of tent stitch, using shiny and matt yarns.

9 A broken coloured tent stitch ground matches the colours in the faceted beads arranged against it.

10 Groups of bugle beads against a horizontal striped background of tent and satin stitches.

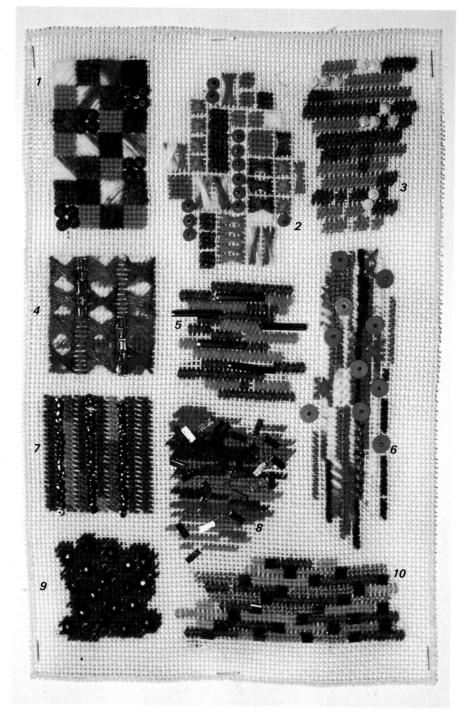

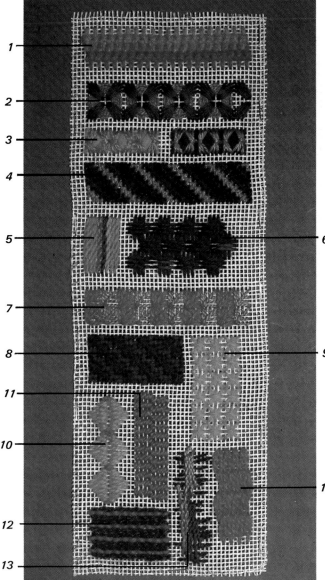

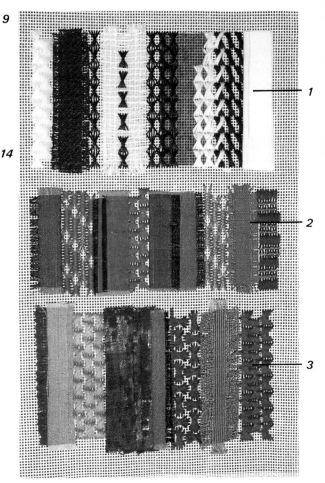

Plate 5—Piping cord covered with close satin stitch to produce raised lines. A tent stitch area, in broken colours has wrapped detached cords crossing it. Piping cords covered in orange, pink, tan and magenta soft cotton are set against satin stitch bands of olive, reddish purple and dull turquoise. Vertical covered cords in the same colour range run against a broken background of coloured shapes in olive wool and lime perlé cotton. The cords are separated in places by broad vertical columns of satin stitch in purple and olive wools, with some lines of tent stitch. In addition narrow bands of squares and rectangles in a variety of colours and yarns are separated by piping cords, covered with close satin stitch.

Plate 6 — Vertical broken rows of tent stitch and satin stitch worked in copper lurex, multicoloured gold rayon with straight binding and gold russia braid.

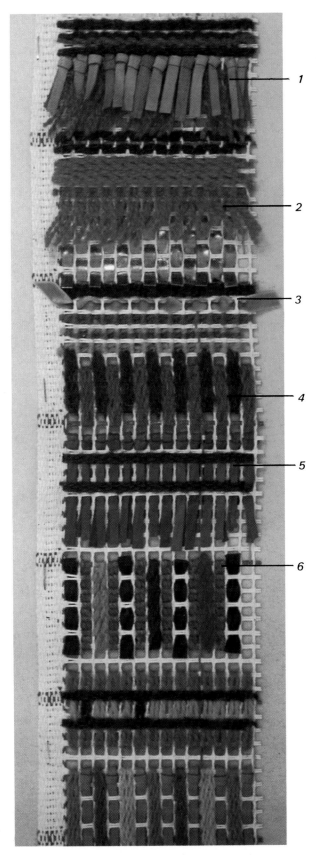

Plate 7 —

1 Rows of stem stitches over leather-looped tassels. Below a wool fringe and four rows of running stitch.
2 Four rows of closely worked stem stitch followed by two rows of back stitch. Looped double threads hang between the stitches to form a fringe. Strips of gold kid are darned through the mesh, leaving exposed threads that form a strong pattern.
3 Rows of stem stitch, threaded ribbon and back stitch with an exposed line of canvas between.
4 Staggered blocks of stem stitch filling one square of canvas.
5 Strips of leather darned through the mesh crossed by rows of stem stitch.
6 Two vertical rows of back stitch on each side of strips of leather with blocks of stem stitch between each strip.

Plate 8—Waterfall.

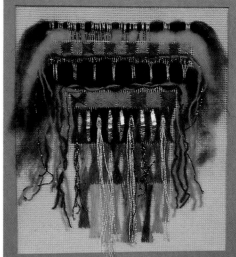

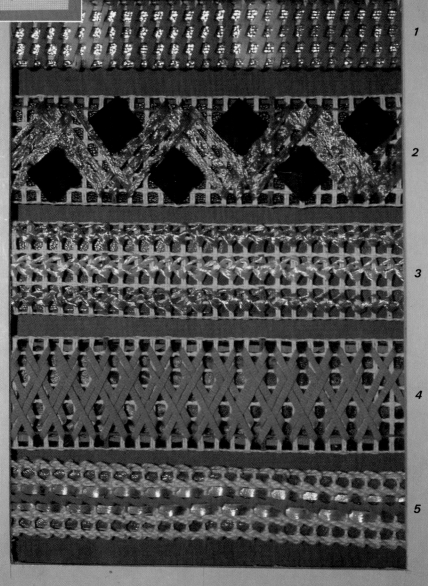

Plate 9—

1 *Blocks of stem stitch
alternately pale blue
and fawn mounted over
a background of silver
leather.*

2 *Interlaced herringbone
stitch worked in tan
raffene, mounted over
black leather. Large
black beads fill the
spaces.*

3 *Rows of open chain
stitch worked in green
and white raffene.*

4 *Two rows of interlaced
herringbone stitch
using turquoise knitting
ribbon, mounted over
black leather.*

5 *Rows of stem stitch in
heavy knitting cotton
and knitting ribbon
mounted over tan
leather. Strips of gold
kid are darned through
the mesh.*

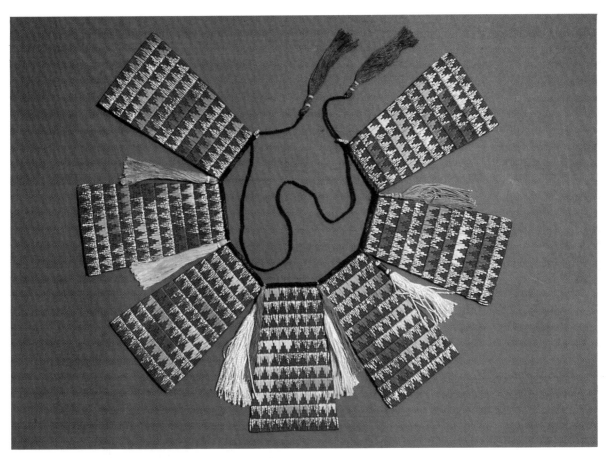

Plate 10 — Necklace in chiffon-covered canvas.

Plate 11 — Animal bins for a child's room.

Plate 12 — Spring Cabbage.

37 Eyelet stitch.

Other yarns, best worked in either long stitches or couching, are those containing metal threads. A wide range in gold, silver and copper is available, and they are exciting to use, adding interest and richness to the work. You can use them to advantage by threading them through foundation stitches, instead of taking them through the canvas.

By handling and using the various threads you will find that you become 'yarn conscious' and will see qualities that previously seemed unimportant. At this point, try to discover more about yarns by making some investigations of your own. Save any scraps of fabric, particularly woollen tweed mixtures. Pull the threads apart and examine them. **Warp** threads from larger pieces may well be used in your work; they are the stronger threads. Yarns used in the **weft** can be more variable as they do not need the strength of the warp and it is they that largely contribute to the textural interest of the cloth.

38 Fishbone stitch in a variety of white threads, which include slubbed knitting yarn, nylon knitting wool, soft embroidery cotton, silk, perlé cotton and silver lurex. The slope of the stitch is varied and is worked vertically, horizontally and on the diagonal over different numbers of threads. Pearl beads add additional interest.

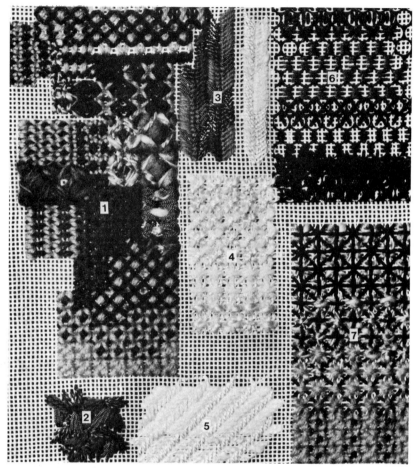

39 (1) A block of rice stitch in shades of blue and olive green in a mixture of yarns: tapestry and Bernat Klein wools, a variegated weaving yarn and a shiny green rayon. The rice stitches differ in scale and shape within the block.

(2) Straight stitches in groups of four radiating from one point, grouped in a random arrangement to form a solid area.

(3) Fishbone stitch in various yarns: wools, perlé cotton and shiny rayon, all in shades of turquoise and green. A second band uses a selection of white yarns.

(4) Double cross stitch in a selection of white yarns including perlé cotton, slubbed weaving yarn, heavy nylon and knitting yarns.

(5) Damask darning using a variety of white yarns.

(6) A band of copper sequin waste held in place by straight cross stitches in olive green, overworked with cross stitches in black; straight stitches fill the spaces in the central band, followed by horizontal darning stitches in groups of three in a chequer arrangement. Diagonal straight stitches in black knitting yarn are followed by pairs of horizontal darning stitches. The final band is velvet stitch with some loops left uncut.

(7) A band of double-cross stitch in shades of turquoise and black using an assortment of yarns, followed by a block of rice stitch using the same yarns.

Clip the yarns that you find interesting to a sheet of card for reference. Untwist these yarns if they are plied. You may find some surprising combinations, which you can use either to produce a colour mix, or to introduce texture with slub yarns. This method of reference is very rewarding and you will discover ideas for mixing your own yarns in the needle. The glint of shiny yarns with wool produces an attractive contrast. Colours may be mixed (*Fig. 39*); a single strand with a heavier yarn will produce an unexpected difference as the result in working is not uniform. It is worth experimenting: being inventive makes your work personal.

Make your own collection of yarns for working from every possible source, even **Christmas wrappings**, when they are available. Keep them in good order, separate the colours in polythene bags for convenience in use. Yarns play a major role in the creation of ideas on canvas, but they do not perform this apart from the canvas that supports them.

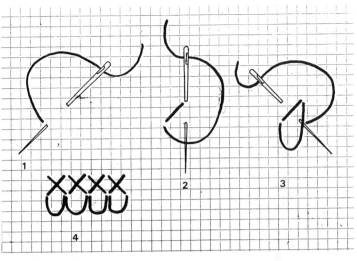

40 *Velvet stitch.*

41 *One inch squares of tent stitch, in shades of grey, using knitting wool, soft cotton and rayon wool mixture, the tones ranging from almost white to charcoal. Superimposed vertical bars of needle weaving in soft cotton and perlé cotton in tones of grey.*

Always consider the scale and colour of the canvas mesh and work your experiments before finalizing your scheme. The canvas can make an important textural contribution. When it is not to be covered completely its colour will be part of the total colour scheme, and yarns should be laid on with this in mind. As your reference material grows, along with experience, you are likely to make reasonable assessments from the start, but you cannot foresee the exciting possibilities that may emerge as a result of your selection of materials and stitches.

It is useful to work a successful idea more than once, varying one of the ingredients, such as colour, relative positions, tones or even the stitches. Turn the worked piece round and look at it from different angles. Always complete an idea; it may not entirely please you but may become a starting point for a second arrangement. Keep everything you work and mount it in your reference file.

Some yarns are ideal for wrapping cords or bunches of mixed threads. The wrapping may cover the whole or part; it is done evenly and at tension, with the thread ends safely secured. The position and contribution of the cord in a design should be planned before wrapping is begun by laying the cord over the worked areas and moving it around until you are satisfied with the arrangement.

Plaits, fringes and tassels have always held a fascination for the textile worker and these are all fully considered in the chapter on texture.

42 Blocks of fern stitch worked mainly horizontally, using a great variety of yarns; the spaces between the blocks are filled with tent stitch. Framed in parisian stitch, the whole is worked in shades of pink and maroon. Designed and worked by Pauli Jennings.

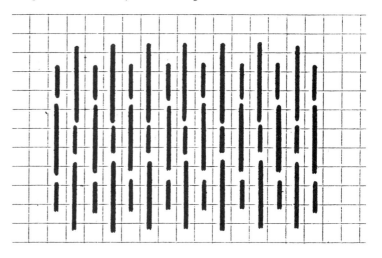

43 Parisian stitch.

44 *A beret with some threads of the canvas withdrawn and bands of needle weaving worked on those remaining. An assortment of ribbons, strips of leather and slubbed Bernat Klein knitting wool, in shades of brown and gold, woven across the area. The spaces filled with rice and cross stitches, all in shades of cream, gold and brown.*

3 STITCHES

Stitches are not creative in isolation – their effect depends on your placing them together skilfully. For example, running stitch with detached chain stitches is an interesting combination. **Running** or darning stitches can be of any length. They may be worked in one size only or alternate with a larger or smaller stitch. If four or more lines are worked the result could be squares, alternating with columns. This in itself could be attractive when related to chosen yarns; you could perhaps work most lines in wool with one only in perlé, giving a shiny glint.

Single chains, each secured independently, are very useful and contrast well with running stitches. They can be worked in any position, vertically, horizontally or obliquely, singly or in groups, regularly or irregularly and can be super-imposed on areas that have been already worked. As the shape of the chain is open, the colour of the darning will show through and that will add interest. The rows of darning could, perhaps, be shiny with the chains in matt cotton or wool. (These may seem small details, but the interest and richness of a design depend on such considerations.) Having worked out one idea, turn the canvas round and look at the work in a vertical position; it may suggest develop-ments. Changing the yarns used, the relative positions of colours and tones and possibly the scale of the same stitches will present an arrangement which will appear quite different.

Use the canvas as you would any other fabric and, where the mesh of the canvas peeps through the stitches, accept it as another ingredient in the pattern. An interesting result can be achieved if

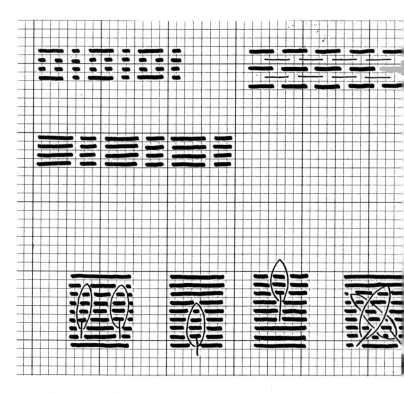

45 (Top) *A block of alternate long and short darning stitches.*

46 (Bottom) *Single chain stitches superimposed on a worked background.*

single threads of the canvas, either vertically or horizontally, are left unworked. This can be done at regular intervals or at random, adding a pleasing lightness to a design. If you have been working in straight rows, try working short rows and move down in steps. It is always a good idea to experiment with placing. Different background shapes may appear as a result. Try working the larger, individual stitches, for example, part-rhodes, in **half-drop formation**. Then experiment with the background and also with the placing of the stitches.

Initially, it is helpful to work with a limited number of chosen stitches, about five or six. Discoveries made from the working of these can be applied to any others made later. Experimenting with scale of stitches, yarns and canvas can lead to some surprises in the effects obtained. For instance, increasing the size of stitch but not changing the yarn or canvas will give a lighter appearance because more or larger areas of canvas will show. Instead of using yarns of uniform thickness, try using a little of a very fine thread. Threads may also be mixed in the needle, matt with shiny, dark with light, bright with muted colours and so on.

When stitches are worked large, there will be opportunities to add further threads by darning under some of the yarns already in place. By laying various colours and types of yarn on the work, you can successfully judge the result.

47 *Wheatsheaf stitch.*

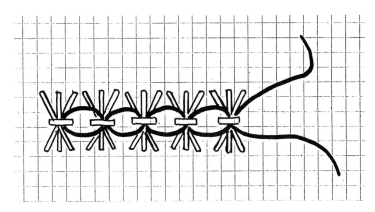

48 *Shell stitch.*

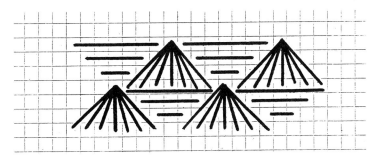

49 *Milanese stitch.*

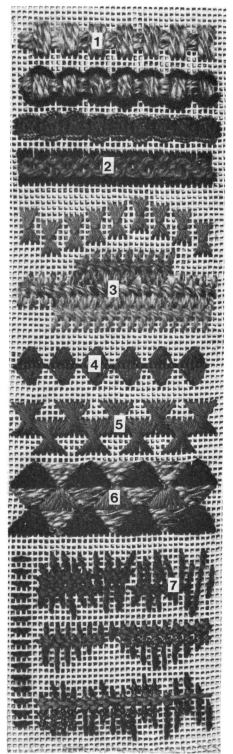

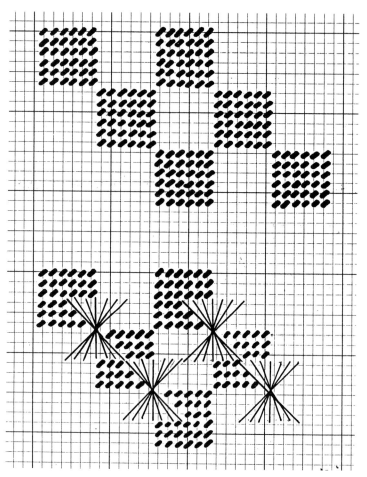

51 Part-rhodes stitch arranged in half-drop formation.

50 (1) First stage of guilloche stitch followed by two completed rows.

(2) Shell stitch based on wheatsheaf which appears on page 39.

(3) Tied-gobelin, the three rows encroaching to form a textural surface.

(4) Rococo stitch.

(5) Part-rhodes stitch arranged so that the stitches encroach.

(6) Milanese stitch producing black and gold triangles with spaces between filled with contrasting yarn.

(7) Irregular and shaped foundation stitches produce free arrangements of raised-chain band.

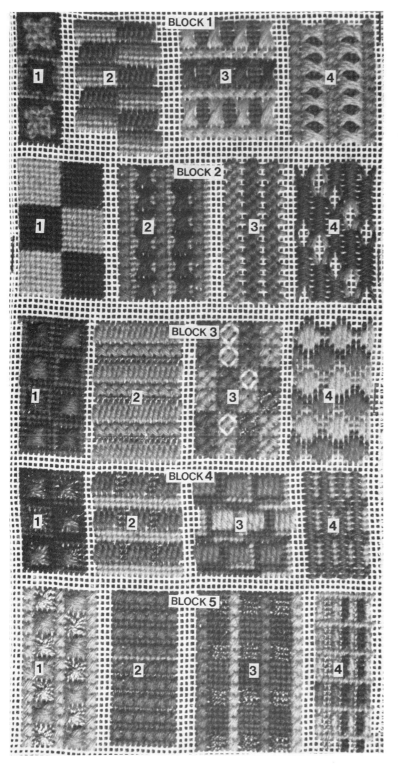

52 Block 1

(1) Interlacing stitch on contrasting squares.

(2) Rows of tent alternating with tied-gobelin.

(3) Part-rhodes in alternate colours, separated by orange tent stitches. Cross stitches worked between rows.

(4) Similar to (3) but worked vertically with rhodes stitches closer together.

Block 2

(1) Squares of tent stitch showing different tones.

(2) A modification of (3) and (4) in block 1 with additional rows of tent.

(3) Three rows of raised chain band.

(4) Spring stitch using contrasting yarns to enclose unworked canvas shapes.

Block 3

(1) Rhodes cushions surrounded by tent stitches in a contrasting colour.

(2) Tied-gobelin in wool, cross stitch in soft cotton, tent stitch in perlé cotton.

(3) Rice stitch using two shades of wool. Perlé cotton used in places.

(4) Satin stitch shapes in contrasting colours and placings separated by small vertical stitches.

Block 4

(1) As in block 3, (1), but using perlé cotton for rhodes stitch instead of wool.

(2) Blocks of tied-gobelin in wool, separated by a vertical block of two tent stitches in perlé cotton and two horizontal rows of tent stitch in wool.

(3) Blocks of four satin stitches, outlined by two rows of tent stitch in varying colours, all worked in wool.

(4) Vertical lines of satin and tent stitch worked in wool of contrasting colours.

Block 5

(1) Rhodes stitches in alternate wool and cotton. Vertical rows of cross in wool.

(2) Horizontal rows of cross in wool separated by lines of tent in various yarns.

(3) Vertical lines of cross with tent between and tied-gobelin at intervals.

(4) Spaced horizontal rows of tent, the areas between filled with blocks of tent and lines of long cross caught down, all in a variety of threads and colours.

Any surface stitch may be used successfully. The mesh of the canvas can be helpful to beginners as the threads of the canvas act as useful guide lines. Similarly, composite stitches – that is, those requiring foundation stitches, such as interlacing or raised-chain band – can be much more readily learned on canvas as the foundation stitches are easily placed. Preparation for **raised-chain band** and **raised-stem band** consists of working horizontal stitches one above the other, spaced regularly (*Fig. 54*). The width will depend on the scale of working. They may be worked to form vertical columns or arranged in a variety of simple shapes. The yarn chosen for this stage is part of the whole and should work well with that used for the chain or stem which follows, as it is not completely obliterated (*Fig. 55*). Test out all possible combinations. Because in the second stage the needle does not pass through the canvas, all kinds of exciting yarns may be used including slubs and metal threads. In the experiments which you work, try several ideas using different yarns and colours, once you have placed the foundation stitches.

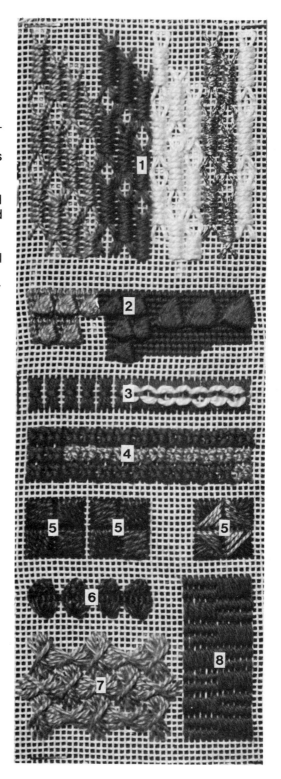

53 (1) A block of spring stitch in an assortment of yarns which includes lurex.

(2) Woven tent stitch in two sizes.

(3) A group of wheatsheaf stitches leaving one canvas thread between each. Threading of the second group forms shell stitch.

(4) Link stitch in two different yarns.

(5) Diagonal stitches to produce reverse cushion stitch, one block having cross corners.

(6) Four rococo stitches.

(7) A block of fan vaulting.

(8) A block of satin stitch in two different sizes.

54

Top right
Tent stitch strips worked in crewel wool arranged freely as a basis for developing a pattern. Connected by horizontal stitches, some worked as raised chain band. Two squares of unworked canvas, together with smaller areas, contrast with the solid tent stitching.

Centre
The tent stitches change in colour and tone, becoming darker and redder towards the base.

The other three examples are worked very freely, making full use of long stitches which sometimes pass from top to bottom. Most are caught down by the horizontal foundation stitches of raised chain band.

55 *The foundation stitches for raised-stem band are shaped to produce a swirling pattern. Those nearer the centre are more solidly worked; some have just a single line.*

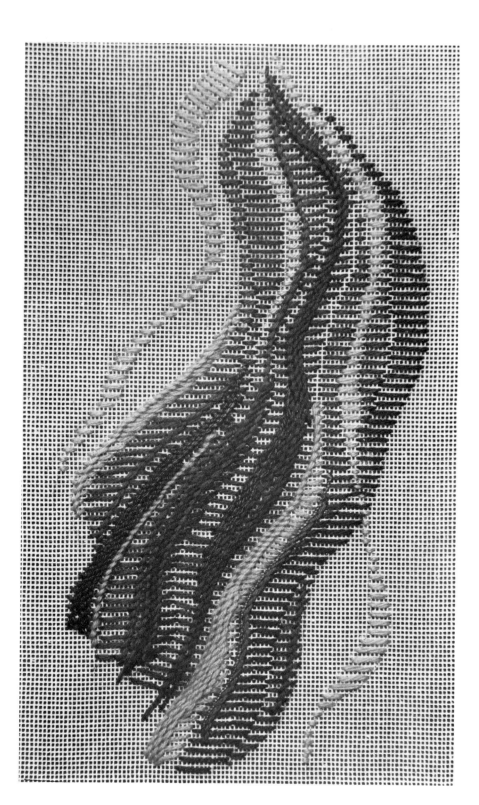

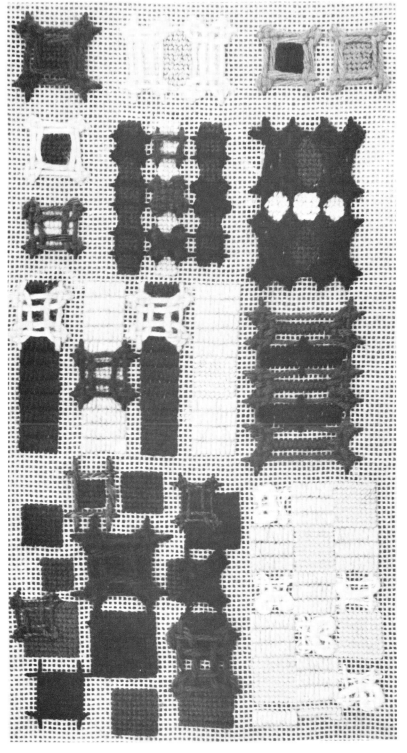

56 Interlacing; this versatile stitch may be worked freely. Combined with other stitches, such as tent and satin, there is scope for changes of yarn. Changes in proportion can be interesting. Note the elongated version (mid-right) worked in gold, soft cotton, the two centre threads overworked in satin stitch with perlé cotton. The intervening background spaces are filled with two rows of black satin stitch with longer central stitches extending the black shapes and securing the long gold threads.

(Below) A complete change of yarn, though not of colour, can produce interesting results. Three different yarns have been used. The matt squares are worked solidly in fine white wool, using tent stitch. Three rows of satin stitch in perlé cotton give a shiny but broken effect. The remaining squares are in contrast using a slub yarn to work the interlacing.

Another stitch requiring a preliminary foundation is **interlacing**, which can form a border or single square of four stitches (*Fig. 58*). On canvas the stitches are easy to place. These must interlace. The fourth stitch, 7-8, slips under the first, 1-2, before going through the canvas. The stitch is traditionally worked as a square, but the proportions of any stitch may be varied and interlacing can be oblong, as shown on the sampler. The lacing may be worked in the same thread or another colour or type. Whichever yarn is chosen will greatly affect the appearance. If it is thick, the rounded corners are solid, and there are only slight peeps of canvas in the centre. If the yarn is fine and tightly twisted, the result is light and lacy, showing its coils. Try it!

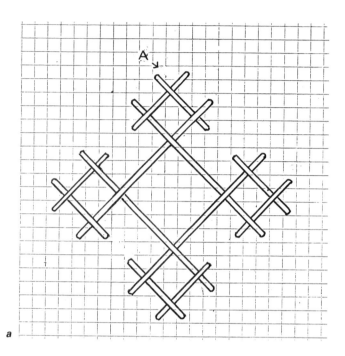

a

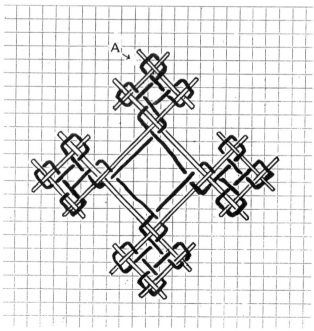

b

57a and **57b** *Interlacing stitch.*

46

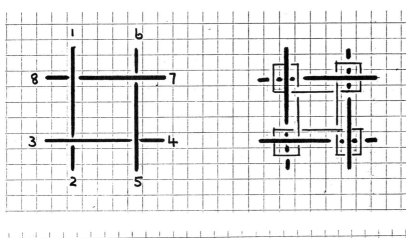

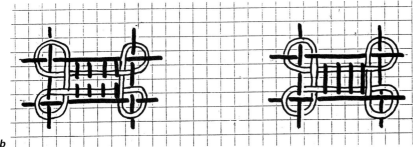

58a and **58b** Elongated interlacing stitch.

Experiment with a variety of yarns as there are many ways in which colour and tones affect the design. For example, if there is to be a small area of tent stitch, a different shade or tone of the same stitch can be used for some of the stitches. Alternatively, the type of yarn can be changed; intersperse a few perlé stitches in the worked area. Such slight changes do not affect the design as a whole but they certainly add interest. Beautiful yarns which would not be seen at their best if worked in small stitches might be laid on the surface and couched down with tiny stitches at intervals. The couching stitch may be more elaborate and play an important part in the design, for example in crossed gobelin stitch.

Some stitches can be worked to fit into the spaces left in previous rows, this is known as **encroaching** and is useful if an area is to be completely covered. Part-rhodes stitch does this very well, particularly if a rich patterning is wanted, for example in evening wear or for a bag.

The textural contribution of stitches can be a very important feature in a design. Some, particularly knotted stitches, can produce attractive contrast, as also does the superimposing of stitches on smoother ones like satin or tent (*Fig. 65*). Then there are the tufted and looped stitches which produce really heavy texture and, where appropriate, add interest or richness. These are turkey rug knot, velvet stitch, Victorian tufting and surrey stitch. Yarns may be mixed as required. When working tufting, a start is always made at the base of an area. Loops may be any length. They may be left as they are or cut to form a pile, according to the effect required. Depth of pile can be controlled and trimmed. Even a single row or a few stitches produce exciting contrasts and focal points. Fringes produce a loose effect, suggest movement, softening and enriching edges.

It can be stimulating to introduce other materials into the work: strips or simple shapes of felt, leather or vilene and also braids and cords. Then there are beads of all shapes and sizes and plastic and metal rings and ones made by buttonholing on a ring of wool. Regard any of these items as starting points and place them on the canvas, perhaps using two together. Move things around and ideas will come, to be interpreted with an assortment of suitable yarns and choice of stitches. All kinds of arrangements will emerge which should be noted

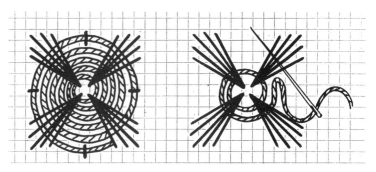

59 *Petal stitch.*

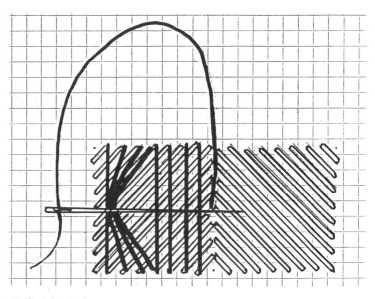

60 *Curtain stitch.*

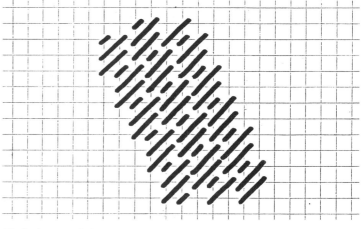

61 *Cashmere stitch.*

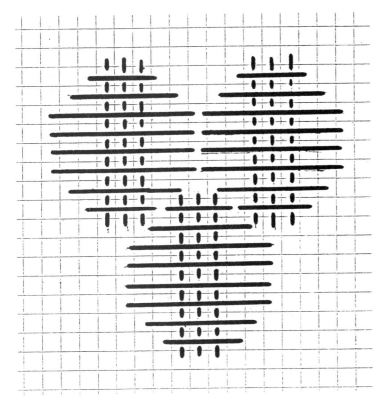

down and then work can begin on one of them. It is when making such experiments that scraps of yarn are useful for moving about in relation to the strip or rings. Decide which areas may need to be worked before attaching the selected item. Strips may be fastened with small, inconspicuous stitches or by others which both fix and contribute decoratively to the result. Rings can be wrapped with yarn or buttonholed. This allows for further stitches to be added across the ring; work any ideas that seem promising and study each stage of the work critically.

62 *Beetle stitch.*

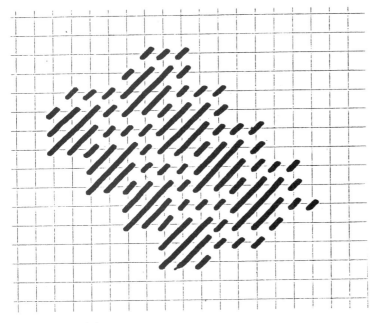

63 *Moorish stitch.*

Do not unpick work when trying small experiments. Decide what you think might improve an idea and then work a second version. *Keep everything* and file it carefully. Good judgement in this, as in everything else, can only develop with experience, and experience can only be gained by *doing*.

64 (1) Cretan stitch with varied spacings superimposed on a background of tent stitch.

(2) Chevron stitch in white yarns of different thicknesses on a tent stitch background.

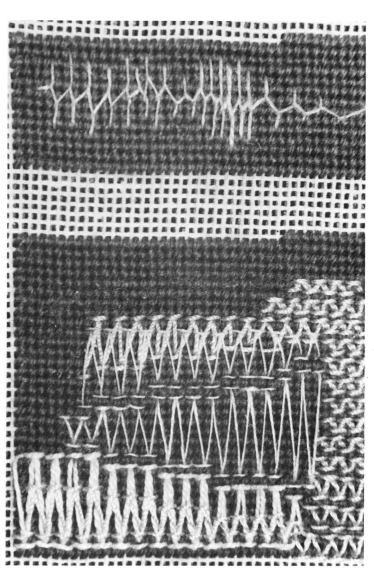

65 Threads withdrawn and bands of needle weaving worked over the remaining verticals. Separated by blocks of long-legged cross stitch.

4 TEXTURE

The term texture describes the surface of things – rough, smooth, knobbly, uneven – and implies a quality of raising above the general level. When used of embroidery, texture refers to the kind of surface created with threads, stitches and any other applied materials. A heavy or light texture can be produced. For example, an area worked with bullion knots (*Fig. 66*) would give a heavy texture that contrasts well with smooth areas of tent stitch. Such contrasts are not dependent on colour changes. Some most attractive designs can be worked entirely in white, when yarns of varying weight and type, matt or shiny, are used and combined with a good selection of stitches. It is important to use white canvas when planning an all-white scheme so that the attractive mesh of the canvas can be incorporated.

Because good textural ideas contribute so much to the richness of embroidery, it is worthwhile experimenting with a variety of yarns, canvas and stitches and assessing the results. Try the same yarn on fine and coarse canvas, using the same stitches. You will find that the yarn lies flatter on the coarse canvas while it sits up on the finer one, creating stronger textural interest. Choice of stitch will be governed by the effect required. Stitches vary in character and some will be more textural than others. The effect will be heightened if they are worked in a tightly twisted smooth yarn, like macramé twine. The only way to develop judgement in these matters is to experiment and learn from results. That is why it is so important to keep all the experiments, as looking at these will suggest other approaches.

66 *Two examples suggested by seaweeds and encrusted rocks.*

(1) *Tent stitch in rich rusts, golds and purples with a few crosses and bullion knots. Unworked canvas breaks up the area of tent stitch. Bullion knots worked on the tent ground and directly on to the canvas in white cotton.*

(2) *Padded suede and silver leather form the centres of the limpet shapes, encircled with bullion knots of varying lengths. The background in shades of gold tent stitch is overworked with white bullion knots in matt cotton. Colours are muted in shades of fawn brown and grey.*

Texture is a most important ingredient in design, as it adds contrast and variety to the surface. Initially its contribution is probably less perceptible than that of colour, but with growing awareness and experience, you will consider it as a matter of course. The heaviest textures are those where rug knots, velvet stitch and surrey stitch are used to produce areas of tufting and fringing (*Fig. 67*). Their use need not be confined to large areas – they can contribute interest with a few stitches in small groups, in a variety of yarns (*Fig. 68*).

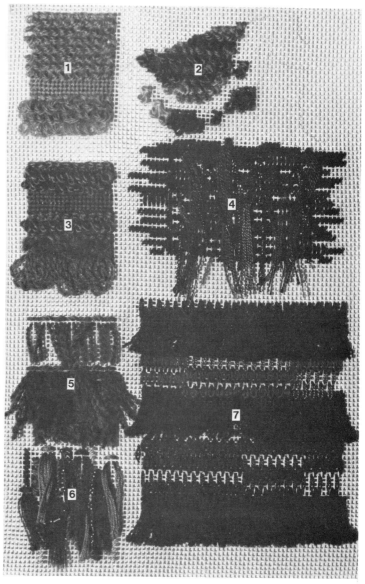

67 (1) *Velvet stitch in wool with bands of tent stitch showing contrast.*

(2) *Velvet stitch.*

(3) *A combination of velvet stitch and tent stitches, with one row of velvet stitch with cut loops.*

(4) *An area of mixed satin and tent stitch leaves unworked canvas threads at intervals. The background is worked first in burgundy, bottle green and dark blue wools. Long tassels in knotted tufting, made of weaving yarns, are inserted, and strings of small beads and bugles hang among the tassels.*

(5) *Another example of knotted tufting in a mixture of rust wool and rayon.*

(6) *Knotted tufting which includes loops of stranded cotton in old gold against olive crewel wool. Strips of gold beads add sparkle.*

(7) *The fringed strips of black upholstery tweed are attached along the top edges with chain stitches. Other chain stitches in brown and purple are spaced to leave attractive unworked patterns in the canvas.*

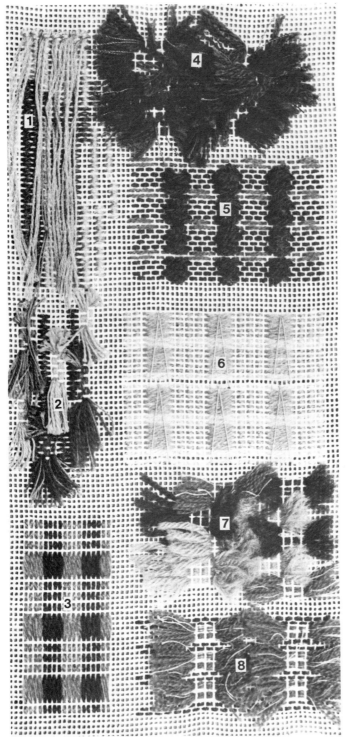

68 White threads of the canvas play an important part in the experiments on this sampler.

(1) Blocks of satin stitch in dark and light tones have knotted tufts made from long lengths of crewel wool and stranded cotton, hanging freely over the blocks.

(2) Bunches of threads darned vertically over four or five threads of the canvas, cut at each end to produce tufts. Horizontal satin stitches, using a mixture of yarns, cross the tufted areas.

(3) A darning pattern in two shades of purple, using stitches of differing length.

(4) A tufted area, mainly of wool, is a horizontal version of **(2)** above.

(5) Another darning pattern in two contrasting colours. The dark coloured row includes a loop between every third stitch, making an interesting surface.

(6) A darning pattern in pink and grey wools, having blocks of three stitches worked over one thread of canvas followed by one stitch over six threads. The unworked threads of the canvas stand out as fine white lines. Over the six-thread wide blocks are two long stitches in orange stranded cotton, forming an inverted 'V' shape.

(7) A similar arrangement to **(4)** above, with different coloured tufts in random groups.

(8) A more regular arrangement of tufts which include a single strand of a contrasting yarn; the tufts are separated by two rows of running stitches. The three white threads of the exposed canvas make prominent vertical lines.

A very simple way of introducing **loops** is to work them along with tent stitch. They may be of any length and placed in any position. Work the tent stitch and at the point required leave a loop (*Fig. 69*), continue in tent stitch until the next loop is to be introduced. The sampler shows variations on this idea which developed from experimenting with the method. Fine yarns of two colours are mixed in the needle to work tent stitch. The alternate rows are gobelin, worked in wool. Long loops are introduced randomly in the rows of tent stitch.

Use the very simplest stitches to produce **changes** in the surface. Using darning stitch, work three stitches over one thread of canvas, leaving one thread of canvas between each. Work one stitch over five threads of canvas leaving one thread, then repeat until you have the length required. Work alongside the first row and continue the rows until an oblong block is completed. The result will be raised bands against a chequered ground. One example can be seen in *Fig. 90* in the chapter on design. There will also be horizontal fine lines contributed by the canvas. It is ideas that count, for the stitch could not be simpler. Although one colour only has been used, a variation in tones occurs as the result of mixing of yarn with the lighter threads of the canvas.

Changes in the surface, creating new textural ideas, may be brought about by the inclusion of other materials, such as cords, beads, rings, manipulated fabrics or leather. The use of any of these can contribute interesting contrasts. They should be considered as part of the scheme along with the yarns which have already been selected.

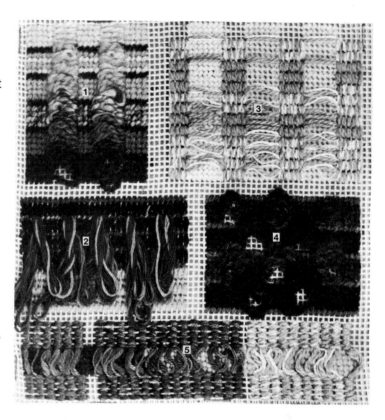

69 Loops of any size may be secured with tent or other small stitches. This sampler gives five different ways where this method has been used.

(1) Blocks formed by four rows of tent stitch, in turquoise carpet wool, followed by long stitches which pass over five threads of canvas. A row of tent stitch in brown separates each development. The next four rows worked in two shades of turquoise with the long stitch replaced by a loop. The block darkens in tone towards the base.

(2) Long slender loops of any length hang over the background which is worked in alternate rows of tent stitch and satin stitch. The loops are formed in the tent stitch row and are separated by four tent stitches. The background, changing in tone, continues beyond the row containing the loops so that they do not hang against unworked canvas.

(3) Three blocks of tent stitch, seven stitches wide are separated by four unworked canvas threads. Varying mixtures of threads, chosen from buff weaving cotton, white stranded cotton and Lystwist (a shiny yarn) make four satin stitches in the unworked spaces, carrying the thread across the tent stitch block. Some variation in spacing.

(4) Similar to (1). Blocks alternate in colour and placing so that there are bunches of threads instead of long tubes.

(5) A central strip of tent stitch, five rows deep, changing in tone along its length. On each side, five satin stitches in contrasting yarns are linked by a loose loop which crosses the central band.

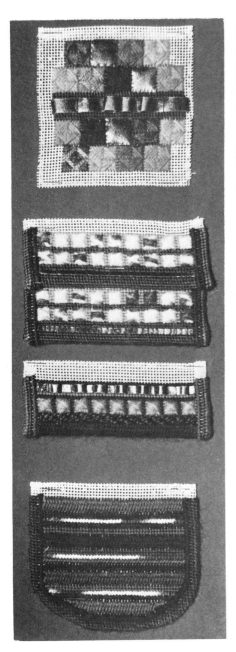

70 Texture experiments for the armadillo described in Chapter 8, Development.

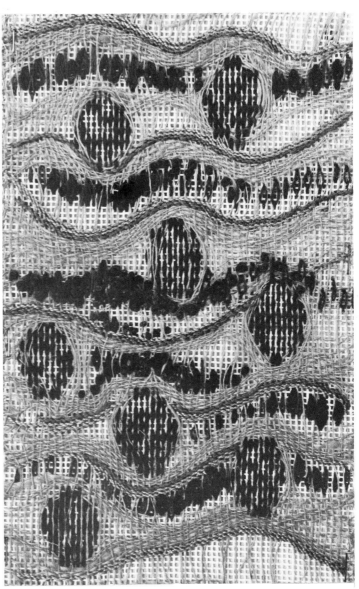

71 Loose scrim applied to the canvas is manipulated with the fingers into waves. Oval spaces appear and are worked solidly in satin stitch in tan wool. Emphasis is given to the edges of the waves by working rows of stem stitch in fawn perlé cotton, french knots and detached chain in shades of tan. Note the unworked white canvas threads.

Cords make a useful contribution texturally, and there is a great variety to chose from (*Fig. 72*). Piping cord, usually white, is attractive in its own right and obtainable in a range of thicknesses. It can also be dyed or wrapped with yarn, matt or shiny. Piping cords may also be used under applied fabrics or in a fold of fabric.

Rayon cords in good colours are also available. A spectacle case is shown (*Fig. 73*) which uses rayon cord in an interesting way. The design of butterflies against triangular shapes was drawn on to the canvas. Starting at the bottom, shiny white cord was laid, one row at a time, so that the design was not obscured. Couching stitches, using blue, black and white stranded

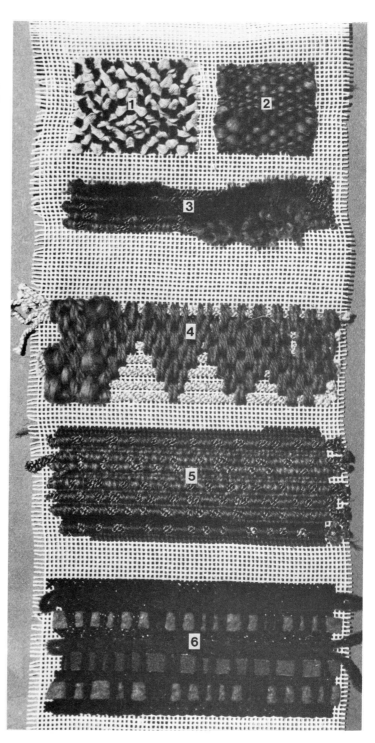

72 (1) and (2) Vertical laid threads, using wool and chenille, in alternate holes of the canvas form a square. Horizontal threads weave under and over the laid threads, going down into the canvas at the end of each row and beginning the next row one hole further down. The weaving thread in block (1) is ric-rac braid and, in block (2) is Bernat Klein knitting wool.

(3) Coloured cords couched onto the background with contrasting coloured wools. Strips of velvet stitch worked between the cords.

(4) Coloured cord, couched onto the canvas with a matching thread. Blocks of burden stitch in contrasting coloured wools and yarns form triangular shapes.

(5) Coloured cords couched onto a background of tent stitch, with varying spaces between the groups of couching stitches.

(6) Strips of felt, suede and chenille, couched down with up and down button hole stitch, using lurex knitting yarn. rows of long-legged cross between each strip.

cotton stitched down the cord, their arrangement building up the design of butterflies, row by row. A change in the spacing of the straight stitches, allowing more or less of the white cord to be exposed, introduced another tone to the colour range. The idea of using rayon cord in this way emerged after studying the 'or nué' technique in goldwork.

Bunches of assorted yarns might be treated as cords. Experiment also with hand-made cords. All produce exciting coils and twists which then suggest ways of placing in a design, perhaps against a background of tent stitch and lines of unworked canvas.

Beads have always had a place in embroidery. They add richness and interest to the work. In this category we include items such as sequins, shisha glass(*Fig. 88*), metal washers, seed heads and hand-rolled beads in felt or leather. Beads combine well with stitches. They should not be used too sparingly as they need to form a considered feature in a design, the varying density producing points of emphasis.

The smaller beads may be freely added to a smooth, worked surface. They can be mixed with stitches such as french knots and bullion knots to build very attractive textural areas, with shiny or matt yarns. Bugle beads and others of distinctive shape may be used in formal arrangements, in columns, bands or encircling simple shapes.

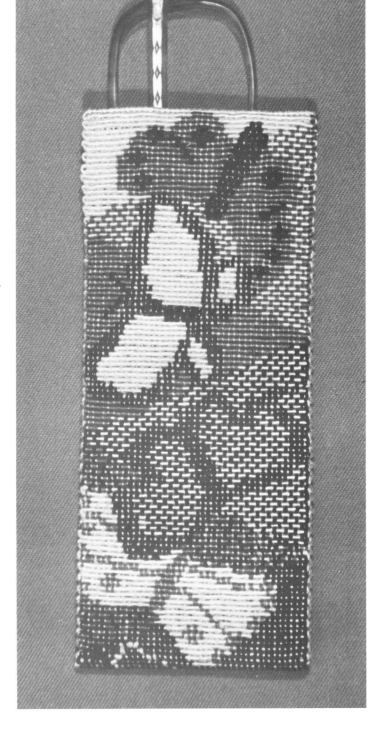

73 Spectacle case, the design of butterflies worked in shiny rayon cord, couched to the canvas using the 'or nué' technique.

Shisha glass, metal washers, large sequins and **large beads** will be a prominent feature in an arrangement and will provide strong shapes and contrasting tones, when combined with the rich textural interest of the stitches.

It is stimulating to experiment with a variety of items, and rings of all kinds suggest fresh ideas. Metal and plastic **rings** may be used as they are, or covered with wrapping or stitchery. Long threads, crossing the rings, give a foundation for woven wheels. If the ring is button-holed, it is then possible to work into both the outside and the inside. Rings of crochet are fun to use as they can be pulled into various shapes and grouped. One idea suggested by this type of ring is to make an arrangement of rings, fasten them down with matching yarn and relate them to the background with a flatter area of stitching. Arrange the rigid type of ring on the canvas, together with selected yarns, until a pleasing design is achieved. You can then see if the rings should be attached and the background worked, or the rings applied to a planned stitched ground. Designs may be horizontal or vertical.

Fabrics contribute to texture in a variety of ways. Ribbons (*Fig. 74*), strips of felt, vilene or even leather can be applied flat, or can be manipulated (*Fig. 75*). They make a good starting point and can result in rich bands of colour when they are

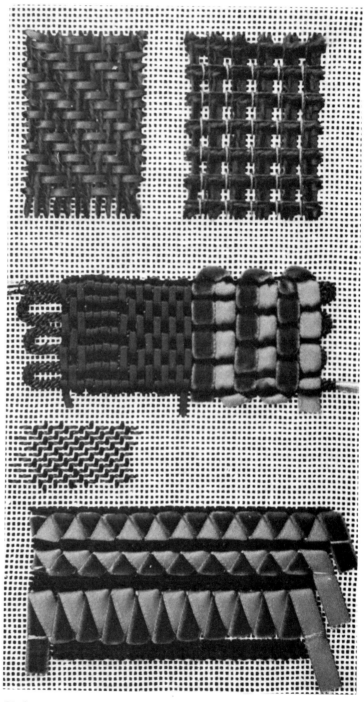

74 *A sampler using ribbons, described in Chapter 8, Development.*

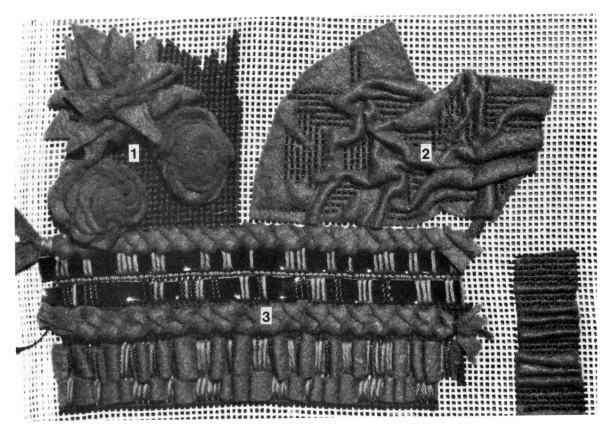

developed with stitches, regularly or irregularly, in a range of yarns.
Padding is another method of achieving changes in a flat surface. Using felt, cut simple shapes of the required size. Next, cut one or two shapes, each slightly smaller than the preceding one. Fix the smallest one first, followed by the middle size, which will completely cover the first. Finally, carefully place the largest one to cover the other two and tack it in place. Secure it with matching small stitches. The colour of the chosen felt will be part of the overall scheme. The padded shape can be developed by your stitching over and around it. Fabrics, including tucks, can be included in a design, and frayed edges add yet another kind of texture. Fringes may be cut from felt and other non-fraying materials.

75 *Triangles and circles of felt in tightly packed clusters applied to a tent stitch background with a single stitch. A piece of felt has been applied with back stitches in straight rows, the felt being ruched between the rows. Plaits made from felt strips, with strips of shiny leather between, are held down by straight stitches in soft cotton and perlé cotton. Strips of felt are stitched down in a similar way, ruched between the stitches.*

Detached strips of needle weaving, caught at each end to form loops, create a dramatic effect against a smooth background (*Fig. 76*). Wrapped cords may be used similarly. Also, the use of **plaits** in design must not be forgotten. First of all try out ideas for the plait itself. Experiment with colour mixing and yarn mixing, weight and type (*Fig. 77*). Usually, plaits are produced by using roughly equal amounts of yarn. Some quite different results come about when proportions are changed so that one strand of the plait is thinner than the other two.

76 A triangular area has horizontal threads withdrawn, needle weaving worked over the remaining vertical threads and an assortment of slub yarns, strips of leather and suede darned under and over the bars. The surrounding areas are shaded from top to bottom, using satin stitch blocks, encroaching gobelin, plaited gobelin and mosaic stitches in shades of gold, blue and brown.

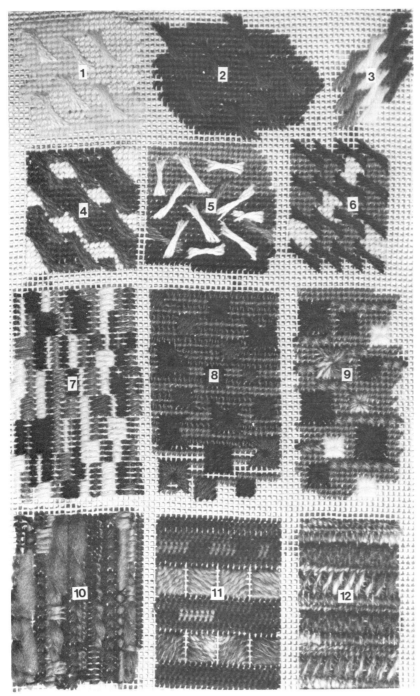

77 The first six examples show different arrangements of part-rhodes stitch on a tent stitch background.

(1) Background in wool and perlé cotton with part-rhodes stitch worked diagonally in the same two yarns.

(2) As in **(1)** but using wool only.

(3) Diagonal stitches encroaching, worked in different shades of wool.

(4) Stepped blocks of tent stitch in white perlé cotton and olive wool, the movement being accentuated by the part-rhodes stitch in pale olive.

(5) A variegated background of tent stitch in shades of yellow, olive and dark green. part-rhodes in pale colours placed at random against the background.

(6) A variegated background in shades of mustard, olive and white wool with part-rhodes stitch in horizontal rows.

(7) Blocks of satin stitch worked over one to four threads in lime green, white, pale olive and brown wools, showing how an interesting surface is created using only one stitch.

(8) Eyelets worked against a gold tent stitch background.

(9) Eyelets against a combined tent and cross stitch background.

(10) Bernat Klein wool, in shades of lemon and olive, is enhanced by vertical rows of cross stitch, satin stitch and tent stitch, in dark brown, old gold and lemon.

(11) Two rows of cushion stitch against a background of tied gobelin; the squares are separated by a single line of unworked canvas. A lemon slub weaving cotton is used for the upper row and a multi-coloured cotton in greys and browns for the lower; the tied-gobelin is worked mainly in brown and olive wool with a little gold as contrast.

(12) Rows of tent, satin and oblong cross stitches using a multi-coloured yarn and old gold rayon.

This can be combined with experiments in colour. Perhaps the thinner strands can also be brighter in colour and shiny in effect. Make some plaits in different tones. When you have an interesting assortment, start experimenting with all kinds of arrangements. Work some vertical columns in preparation for this. Ensure that parts of the canvas are left unworked, not only for the attractive contrast of the mesh but because the textural contrasts will be even stronger.

We have concentrated here on the use of texture in design. Ways of developing textural ideas on the canvas have been suggested which will provide further experience in this field.

5 COLOUR

Everyone responds to colour and everyone enjoys using it; however, it is not always used to good effect because the importance of tone values, contrasts, subtleties and proportion is often misunderstood. Good judgement can only develop with experience and critical observation.

First consider **tone values**. It is, perhaps, simpler to understand tones and their use in terms of black and white. When an illustration or poster is said to be 'black and white', we probably do not mean that literally. There may be many greys between the two, starting with the palest of greys, which are almost white, and going through to greys which are almost black. This is easy to see; what may be more difficult is the translation of tones into multi-coloured schemes (*Figs 78 and 80*).

It is both interesting and enlightening to try out some exercises, first in paper and then in yarns. Cut out templates in thin card, about 2.5 cm square (1 in.). Find as many greys as possible in flat colour from a suitable magazine. Use one of the card shapes as a pattern, draw round it and cut out the greys you have found; include a blackish and a whitish grey. There should finally be about 12 pieces; arrange them in order, starting with the palest and working towards the black. Paste all 12 down on the left side of a sheet of paper.

From your collection of coloured papers, select one colour and cut pieces, matching the grey ones in size in a variety of tones, from light to dark, starting with white. Half close your eyes when judging the tones so that you are seeing depth of tone rather than colour. This is

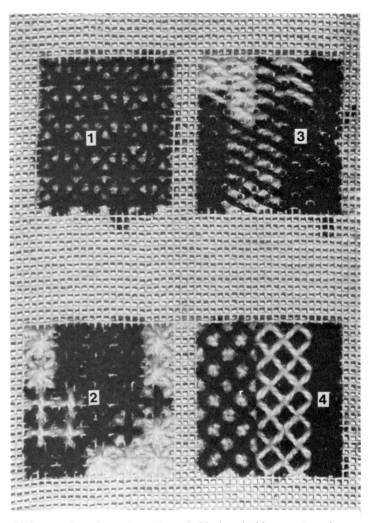

78 An exercise using extreme tones in black and white carpet wool.

(1) A grid of laid threads with four threads of canvas between each vertical and horizontal in white wool. Black wool crosses worked at each intersection over two threads of canvas. Between each vertical and horizontal thread large upright crosses in black wool are formed.

(2) Double cross stitch, some all white, others all black or a mixture of the two.

(3) Long horizontal cross stitches, four threads by two in black and white wool and black raffene.

(4) Rice stitch using black and white wool to demonstrate changes in tone.

79 Double cross stitch.

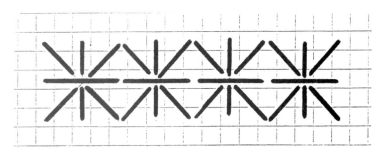

80 A geometric design by Hanni Fletcher in shades of blue and yellow, worked entirely in rice stitch, showing subtle variation in tones.

intended to help your colour perception and, if you find it useful, more columns in other colours could be added. Finally, paste them down and add them to your reference collection.

Other useful experiments concern the analysis of colour. For these, either in paper or in yarn, make a study of one colour at a time. For example, gather together any types of blue yarn which are different in tone. Go on collecting over a period. Then try to discover what might be called a standard blue, neither leaning to green nor to purple. Place this at the head of a sheet. Judge the rest of the colours for their quality of 'greenness', however slight, moving nearer and nearer to turquoise but not beyond. Make a column of these, starting with the purest and moving down to the greenest. Start a fresh column with the rest, beginning with the purest and moving gradually down to those which are just short of purple. This exercise may be carried out with any other colour.

Red may move towards orange or towards purple; orange towards yellow or red. Yellow may move towards orange or green; green towards yellow or blue; and purple towards red or blue.

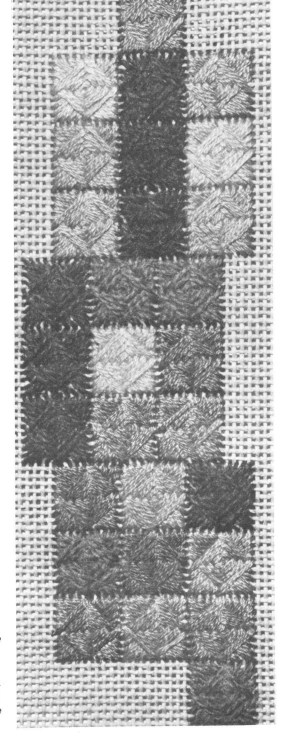

81 *An arrangement of three large squares containing nine small ones, the centre square being out of line but contained by the three darkest squares which lead the eye back to the dark squares in the bottom square. There is no change of stitch, yarn, texture or scale. It depends entirely on colour and the arrangement of tones. Norwich stitch worked in three strands of cotton.*

If you save every scrap of yarn, your collection will be valuable but only if it is kept in order. A simple way to do this is to sort the colours and keep each on a separate strip of card, roughly 20 x 5 cm (8 x 2 in.), with slits cut at intervals in opposite sides. If you have a large quantity, separate colours into polythene bags; they will then be useful for reference and can be pulled out, used to test possible colour schemes and replaced afterwards. They can also be laid on the work in progress, to judge effects. Near tones of colour in a design will tend to merge but will be more interesting than a single colour; extremes of colour act as focal points.

Next consider the proportion in which colours are used in a design. It is helpful to wind yarns round a strip of card in the intended proportions, dealing with not more than five at a time; then consider how they look. The dominant colour may well take up more than half the space in the trial sample, but it need not necessarily be worked in one area, nor will it exclude the use of a little of some of the other colours, by line or spot. Some colours may be in a contrasting type of yarn. You will find that just one strand of stranded cotton can be telling in a scheme.

Remember also that **contrast** in tones is necessary. One scheme might be chiefly in muted shades, with a touch of clear, bright colour. Another might make use of black and white, with two or three shades of one colour, and so on. Good contrasts, in the proportion used can make a tremendous difference. Even after work has begun, watch the effect of colour and stitches as the colour may appear to change in juxtaposition with other shades (*Fig. 81*).

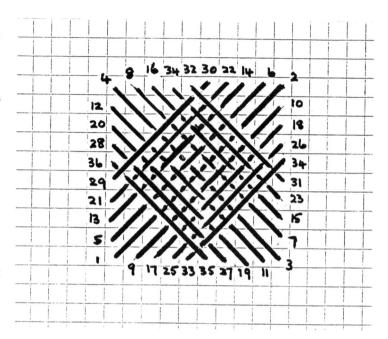

82 *Norwich stitch.*

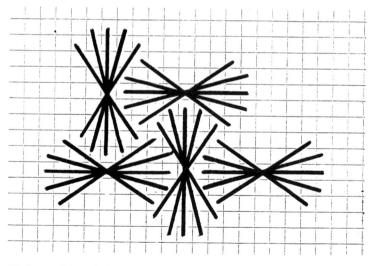

83 *Fan vaulting stitch.*

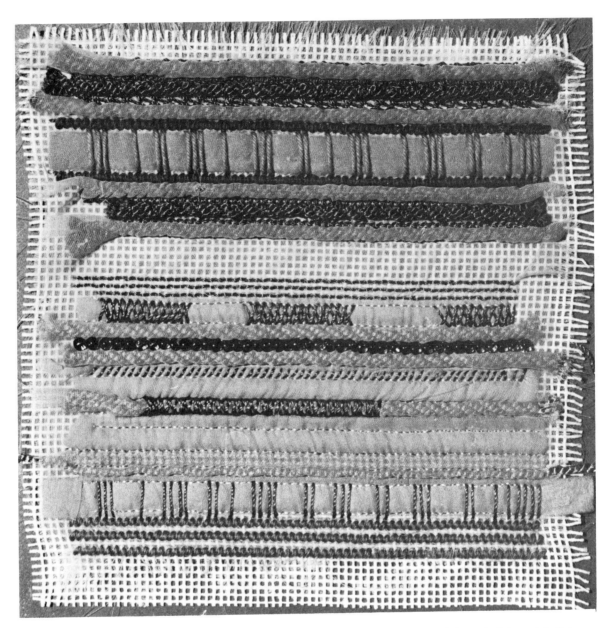

84 *(1) Coloured chiffon laid over ribbons and cords. Tent stitch and long-legged cross stitch worked through both layers, using perlé cotton.*

(2) Coloured chiffon laid over the canvas, held in place by rows of back stitch. A strip of coloured felt under the chiffon has double back stitch worked over it in places. Two coloured cords are covered with chiffon separated by a row of beads. Strips of felt under the chiffon are held down with back stitches and straight stitches.

Juxtaposition is the term used to describe the placing of colours in relation to others. White looks even whiter next to black; black looks ever blacker on white. In other words, strong contrasts accentuate differences and are one way of achieving a focal point in a design.

Colour is affected by the type of yarn used. Matt wools absorb the light; shiny yarns (perlé, raffene, silk) reflect – as do shiny beads.

85 Coloured cords covered with pale pink chiffon and attached to the canvas with back stitches form the tree shape. The foreground is a slubbed thread couched in various colours. The sky is in tent stitch, worked both under and over the chiffon.

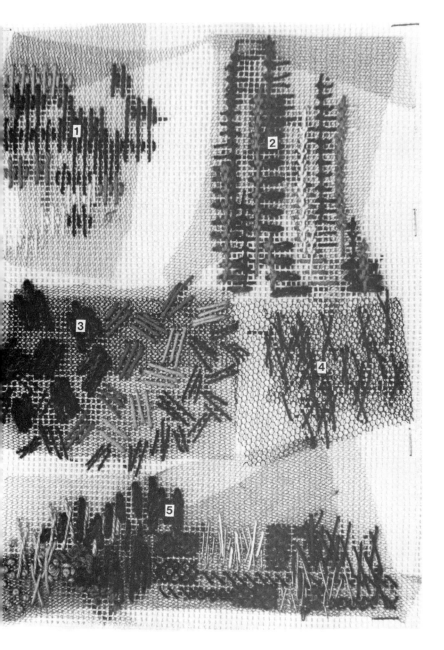

86 *(1) A variety of nets, in green, black and brown, used singly or in layers, change the background colour in addition to adding textural interest. The mesh of the canvas can be clearly seen for working. Large and small stitches in soft and perlé cotton in tan, brown, black, gold and white are used on fine brown net folded to produce a double layer at the top.*

(2) The fine brown net is again used. Horizontal foundation stitches for raised-chain band in tan, white and brown wool and perlé cotton, vary in width and weight and produce a slight curve towards the base. Loop stitches in light tan predominate with a few in brown and black perlé cotton. The white perlé cotton therefore stands out.

(3) Black net is used double in the top half. Groups of two or three stitches are worked in all directions in weaving cotton, soft cotton and fancy wool yarn. Colours light and dark old gold and browns.

(4) Coarse black net, worked in irregular long crosses, using brown weaving yarn and black perlé cotton.

(5) Fine green and brown nets, overworked with rice stitch, french knots, long crosses, cross stitch and vertical stitches.

87 *(1) With four strands of wool in the needle and the darkest shade used first, pattern darning is worked across the width; one strand of dark is replaced by one of light until the final row becomes all light.*

(2) Damask darning is worked from light to dark by the mixing of strands of wool in the needle.

(3) Shaded satin stitch is produced by colours being mixed in the needle.

(4) Another example of pattern darning with the colours mixed in the needle.

(5) Rows of herringbone stitch shading from dark to light.

(6) Rice stitch shading from dark to light by the colour of the underlying cross stitch and the tying stitches being changed progressively.

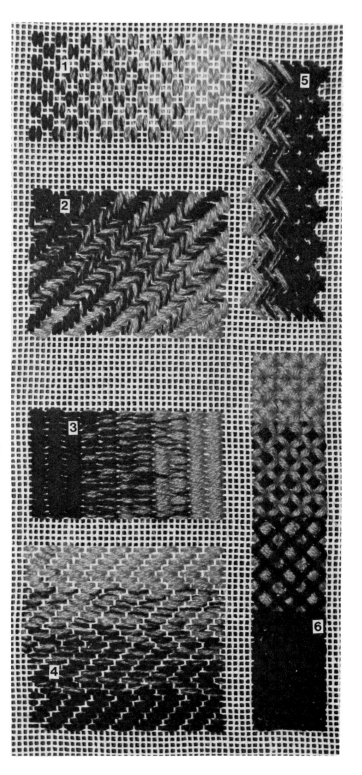

It is interesting to experiment with **transparent** fabrics: net, chiffon and organdie. These not only change the texture but also the colour. The canvas mesh shows clearly through the fabric, and stitches contributing strong texture are very attractive on this background. The transparent fabrics can also be tucked and enclose piping cords. We show some examples of the effects obtained (*Figs 84, 85 and 86*).

Next think about **colour mixing**. With such a wide range of colours to choose from, why do you need to mix colours at all? What is known as broken colour relies on colour mixing in the eye. The result of this is much more lively than flat colour and can be obtained by introducing a second colour in the form of spots, dashes or even whole lines interspersed with the main colour. Stitches that readily encroach into preceding rows are useful in producing a similar result.

Threads of different types, colours and tones may be mixed in the needle (*Fig. 87*), which must accommodate them comfortably to avoid damage. Some very interesting experiments may be carried out and the results will be enhanced if some plain areas are included as part of the design.

Finally, materials other than yarns can contribute colour to the work, and it is worth while trying out some ideas using them. The wide range of colours obtainable in felt makes it an exciting ingredient. The contrasting surface of leather, which is available in a wide range of colours as well as metallized (silver, gold, copper and bronze), can bring interest and richness to the work. Leather and felt can both be cut to give a sharp line, adding crispness to the design. Felt or leather fringes are distinctive in character and bring a pleasant contrast to the embroidery.

By their infinite variety in form, size and surface texture, beads add colour and sheen at the same time as changing the surface. They blend with highly textured stitches, bringing added interest and they look equally well when introduced into rich fringes.

6 DESIGN

There are good and poor designs, interesting and dull ones. Technique is not unimportant, but satisfying and lively designs only develop from good, individual ideas. Beginners appear to become alarmed at the mention of design, but the word simply means a planned arrangement of fabric, threads and stitches. Initially, we shall be using the materials themselves to produce simple but satisfying patterns.

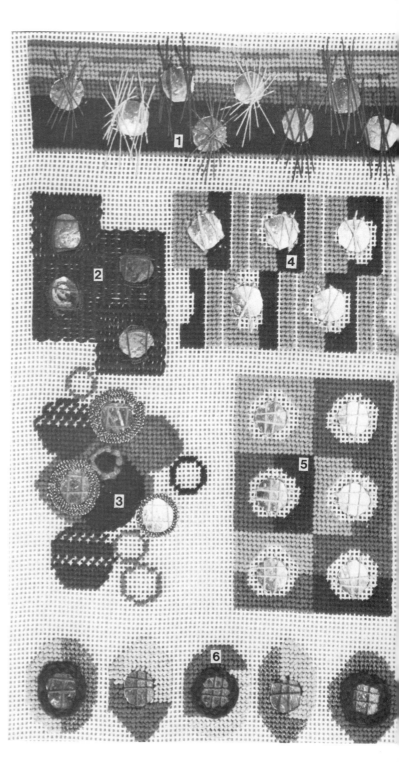

88 (1) *The border encloses shisha glass with closely worked rows of tent stitch, starting with strong pink leading to deep reddish purple. Irregular long stitches in perlé cotton criss cross the glass, being caught down at the edge.*

(2) *Half drop blocks of satin stitch and tent stitch, changing direction for each square, provide the background for shisha. Button hole stitches are worked over the straight stitches holding the glass.*

(3) *A design based on circular shapes with solid tent stitch, rings and shisha glass, attached with coton à broder and surrounded with lurex.*

(4) *Divided squares in grey and brown are worked in tent stitch. Between the squares are vertical rows of white canvas. Shisha glass in the centre of the squares is secured by grey perlé cotton.*

(5) *In the centre of each square, a piece of shisha is secured with four straight stitches in pink perlé cotton. Some unworked canvas surrounds each. Each square is worked in two colours.*

(6) *A row of irregular shapes, in tent stitch, using different greys in perlé and soft cotton. In the centre of each a piece of shisha is secured with four stitches. Alternate pieces are encircled by pekinese stitch in brown soft cotton.*

In the simplest arrangement there is scope for the exercise of the essential elements of design. The main ingredients have already been considered separately in previous chapters, and the next step will be to bring them together.

One of the most important considerations is the need for **contrasts** in the proportions of shapes, colours, tones and textures used (*Fig. 88*). Contrasts are essential in lively design. Uniformity suggests the mechanical, and the result is lifeless. For example, backgrounds required to appear as one colour in a design, on closer inspection, can reveal slight changes in colour or yarn, in the form of spots or dashes. You could, for example, use a contrast of perlé on wool. It is such detail that adds interest and enriches the work.

Variety is an essential element, so yarns of different thicknesses, dull and shiny should be available. In selecting colours, remember the value of tones – they are almost as important as colour itself. Arrange to include the mesh of the canvas as part of the design (*Figs 89 and 90*) by leaving some horizontal or vertical threads unworked. The sampler in *Fig. 91* is worked entirely in a variety of white yarns and pairs of holes in the canvas form an integral part of the pattern in the bottom two blocks. An even more striking contrast is achieved in the pin-cushion (*Fig. 92*) where the unworked squares of the mesh make an attractive chequer design with the blocks of satin stitch,

89 *A variety of stitches are worked over copper coloured sequin waste using black, gold and tan stranded cotton, soft embroidery cotton and wool. The stitches include running, herringbone, cross, satin and tufting.*

needle weaving and backing fabric. In the norwich stitch sampler (*Fig. 93*) two features in this simple arrangement add to its interest: firstly, incomplete stitches contrast with the totally filled squares; secondly, the resulting unworked triangular and diamond shapes catch the eye.

When planning designs the solidity of some stitches needs to be considered; leaving unworked shapes and changing both yarn and scale can contribute greatly to a lightening of the overall effect. This is demonstrated in *Fig. 94* where the attractiveness of the mesh of the canvas is seen as shapes or lines. In another sampler (*Fig. 96*) alternate vertical bars of white canvas make an interesting contrast with the cushioned effect of the stitches. In the block below, larger areas of canvas have been left unworked, creating a lighter appearance. The next sampler (*Fig. 97*) contains horizontal and vertical lines of canvas left unworked, making a clear contrast with the solidly worked shapes. Note also the free treatment of the edges and how this has been achieved. At the bottom of the sampler are two examples, each worked in the same stitch, crossed-gobelin, showing that further variety may be discovered by experimental placing. When working on rug canvas, the spaces opened up are much larger and strips of fabric, ribbon or leather may be placed behind.

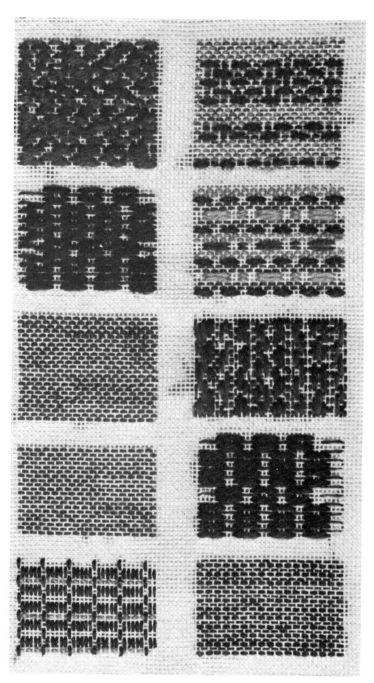

90 *A sampler showing the many variations possible when using running and satin stitches. Different weights of wool are used. Note the contribution made by the unworked canvas; sometimes it appears as horizontal bars, sometimes columns of squares. Endless variations are possible using this simplest of all stitches.*

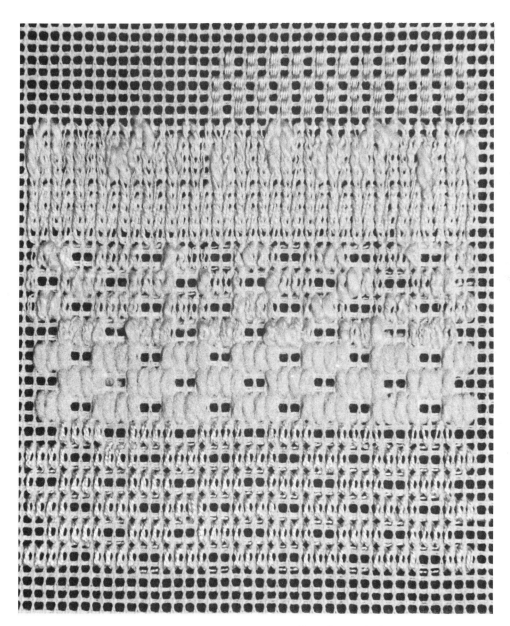

91 Sampler worked entirely in white yarns showing the effect of unworked canvas.

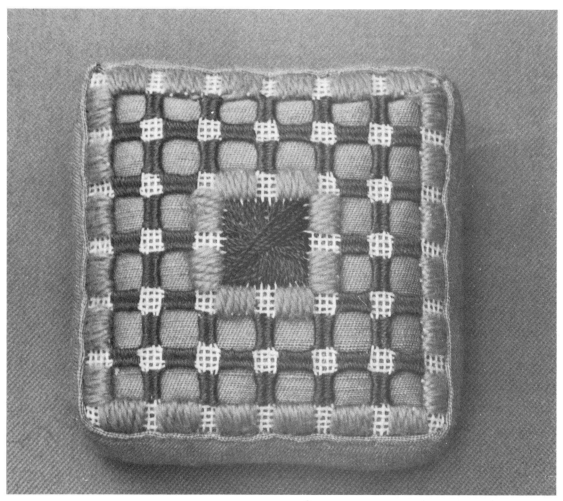

92 A pincushion with a large rhodes stitch in the centre which is surrounded by blocks of satin stitch in wool, leaving squares of unworked canvas. Threads are removed horizontally and vertically around the square and needle weaving is worked on the remaining threads. Blocks of satin stitch alternate with squares of unworked canvas round the edge. A green furnishing fabric provides a background for the squares where threads have been removed.

93 Norwich stitch and part-norwich with unworked canvas shapes included as part of the design. Soft embroidery cotton is used for all the blocks, giving a crisp, sculptured look.

Ideas for design may come from other techniques in embroidery, and blackwork on canvas can produce unusual and attractive results. The stitches need to be worked regularly, but yarns and scale may vary and so may the amount of unworked canvas. In the blackwork sampler (*Fig. 98*) see the central pattern – note how the depth of tone increases towards the base. This result has been achieved by the inclusion of two extra stitches per unit. Tonal contrasts are strong in the square example (*Fig. 99*). The eye goes directly to the almost white centre and then immediately out again to the four dense black blocks, between which a small repeating pattern shows horizontal and vertical blocks of unworked canvas. Solid triangles of tent stitch complete the inner square and lead to tufted corners which contribute textural richness. A second pattern, more closely stitched than the other, gives the right tone to support the dark corners.

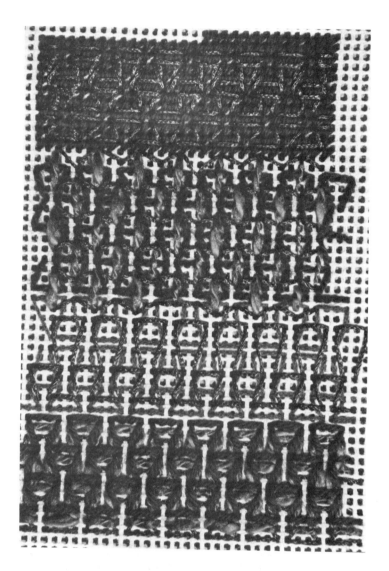

94 *A sampler showing Japanese darning worked in a variety of yarns and, in the first rows, against a background of tent stitch. The unworked bars of the canvas add prominent lines to the pattern.*

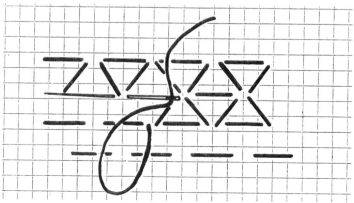

95 *Japanese darning.*

78

96 A sampler showing a block of stitchery worked in shades of red, pink and burgundy which relies on the unworked canvas shapes and lines for its pattern quality. A variety of yarns have been used – soft embroidery cotton, perlé cotton and embroidery wools – to work part-rice stitch and satin stitches. The first block contrasts with the adjacent one, worked in greens and fawns, again using rice and satin stitches but having no unworked areas.

This attractive example gave rise to the well-designed shopping bag (*Fig. 100*). Note that the area is divided vertically into three parts, the central band dominating the softer looking and narrower side panels. The blackwork squares and roundels become progressively darker towards the base. Added to this are unusual, pleasing shapes linked to the roundels by crosses. Those who feel doubtful about their ability to design should feel encouraged by this simple and successful layout and try similar projects.

The three bangles (*Fig. 101*) also use counted thread patterns. Beginners may like to try one of these or a pincushion to gain practice on a small item.

Two other pincushions with simple designs are shown in *Fig. 102* and *Fig. 103*. The rectangular design consists of multicoloured squares of mosaic stitch, the direction of the stitch being changed in a random fashion. A variety of threads and colours are introduced, and the word 'PINS' superimposed on the mosaic stitch background.

The second pincushion, in the shape of a shell, is worked mainly in tent stitch with a variegated cotton thread. Occasional patches of surrey stitch and french knots in brown introduce textural interest. The firmness of the canvas helps when making three-dimensional forms, as the shape is held without additional stiffening.

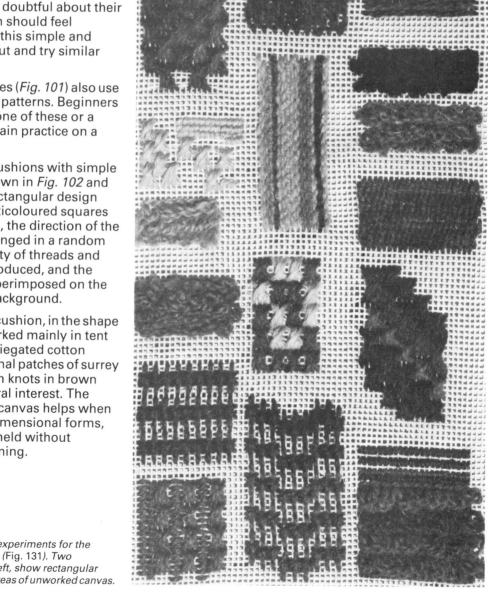

97 A sampler with experiments for the folding chair design (Fig. 131). Two examples, bottom left, show rectangular shapes formed by areas of unworked canvas.

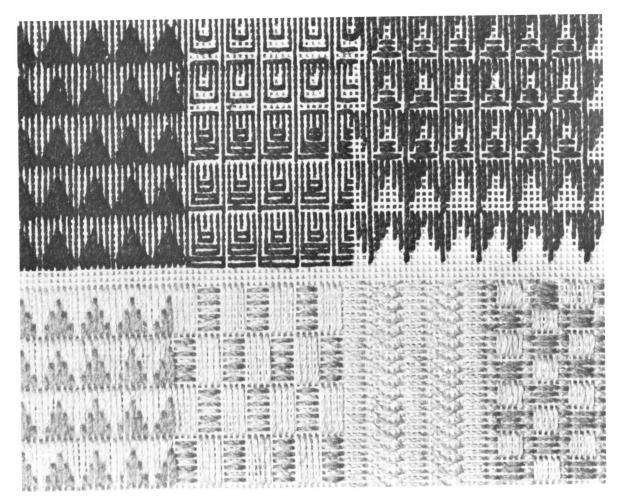

98 *Blackwork sampler.*

As has been suggested elsewhere, it is a good idea to cut out shapes in paper and move them around, trying different arrangements. Always look at the background spaces for they are as important in design as the selected motifs. The first experiments may be worked in horizontal rows, producing bands or blocks, using two or three stitches. Begin by laying the yarns on the canvas so that, eventually, one of them becomes dominant and produces a focal point.

99 Blackwork sampler.

Try a variety of ideas, noting down the most interesting before removing them. Work enough of each idea to see the interaction of the colours, the effect of dark and light and the part played by exposed threads of the canvas; also consider whether enough attention has been given to variation in the proportions of colour, tone and stitches, so that there are points of emphasis. If there is a battle for dominance, the result could be unpleasant or dull. It is a good idea to work a satisfactory pattern more than once, changing the position of tones or proportion of colours and yarns used. Keep all the worked experiments carefully, so that effects may be studied and compared.

You might find it stimulating to include other materials in further experiments, such as felt squares or strips, rings covered or plain, beads and so on. Place the selected items on the canvas and, as before, lay on chosen yarns which will develop the strips or rings and also link them into the border or block. Try as many ideas as possible before actually working a few of them. Making judgements on the effects obtained, without necessarily stitching them each time, is an important stage in developing awareness, and it will be found to be more and more valuable. Look critically as the ideas develop and do not be too committed to preconceived plans.

Work **vertical** columns as a change from the horizontal. These could be exciting rich bands of colour, possibly including some lurex. They will be the main feature and will require a low key background, perhaps relying on texture only. The success of such an effect would depend on the careful choice of colour and tone.

101 Bangles.

If a design is seen not to work in these small experiments, try to discover the cause and work it again. Are dramatic extremes of tone in the right place? Are all the colours, although different, of medium tone only? Half close your eyes and see if the focal point of the design is working. Your critical judgements in these matters will develop and once gained will lead to your handling materials more confidently, adding to the enjoyment of it all. **Variations** in the placing of the dominant features can produce entirely different effects. If you have worked four or five identical rows exactly under one another, the result will show as squares or columns against the background. This pattern can be changed by a different placing of the square. Alternate rows can move the square to the right in working, creating a zig-zag. Or if you move each square further to the right in each succeeding row, you will produce a diagonal effect.

You will realize from these experiments in placing that the possibilities are limitless and exciting. Some of the larger individual stitches – for example, part-rhodes – lend themselves to yet another kind of arrangement. It is known as **half-drop**, where alternate columns of stitches begin half a stitch lower. It is rewarding to experiment freely with placing, and look at the changes that come about as a result. It can produce a different relation between stitches and unexpected shapes of unworked canvas. Such changes cannot be foreseen, and it is this that makes experimenting so worthwhile. Every new idea should be tried out. Mounting and carefully filing everything for reference and comparison is both stimulating and encouraging.

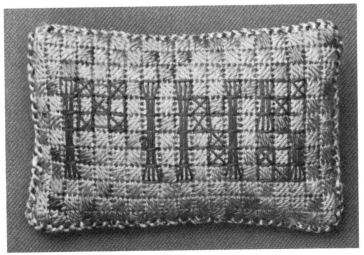

102 Pincushion worked entirely in mosaic stitch in stranded and perlé cotton (shades of grey, pink and purple). Some squares overworked in a darker colour to form the word 'PINS'. Back and front are joined by an edging of raised chain band.

103 Pincushion in the shape of a shell, worked in tent and gobelin filling stitches; it is made with variegated knitting cotton in shades of beige and brown. Some areas of surrey stitch, double-cross stitch and french knots in dark brown stranded cotton, the shape outlined with a narrow line of raised chain band.

What is there to be gained by incorporating other techniques into the work? Each technique has its own special character and it could therefore add enriching contrasts to a design. Some readers are already skilled in other crafts, for example, knitting, crochet or macramé; small pieces from any of these techniques might prove valuable starting points, extending still further the freedom of approach. Consider selected pieces as part of the design from the outset and place them on the canvas, along with selected yarns, so that various positions can be tried out (*Fig. 104*).

104 *A block of log-cabin patchwork in shades of blue, applied to canvas and surrounded by horizontal rows of cross, tent and long-legged cross stitches, worked in a variety of yarns. Some areas of surrey stitch provide tufted strips. The colours of the worked strips repeat the log cabin patchwork colours.*

Fabric-covered card, with or without padding, can contribute a distinctive and strong contrast. Appliqué, according to the fabric used, adds a different surface quality and may also be manipulated, producing strong textural contrasts. *Fig. 105* shows a cushion which incorporates a patchwork effect. The rectangular areas of worked canvas alternate with patches of similar weight in upholstery fabric. The upholstery fabrics should be assembled first, and then the working yarns related to them. Sample pattern books could be used to provide fabrics of similar weights and related colours. Such a cushion could be worked with a group of beginners as a communal exercise.

Another cushion (*Fig. 106*) made using a patchwork technique has small worked squares of canvas, designed to use different arrangements of the same stitches and with a different combination of the chosen colours (shades of green and blue). It was useful to be able to move the individual squares about, until a satisfactory arrangement emerged before joining them together with back stitches.

A piece of knitting, in fine yarn on very large needles will produce a net-like fabric, allowing both canvas and stitchery to show through. It has an elastic quality and so can be pulled into a variety of shapes. As always, one idea will spark off another, and using different materials is always stimulating.

Discs of crochet are attractive in a design as special features. Worked in metallic yarns they will produce a rich addition to your stock of materials. Later, they may be incorporated into evening bags and items such as belts.

Good original design will be further stimulated by an increasing awareness of the quality of **shape**. Both line and mass are needed and there are many sources which can yield fresh ideas. Keep a pad and 3B or coloured pencil handy for noting down interesting shapes. When recording shapes you see, it may not be always practicable to cut or tear them out, but when it is, it is helpful to do so. The only tool needed is a pair of scissors (kept for paper); use these freely, cutting straight into the paper, without previously drawing the shape. Avoid mechanical means of producing an outline, such as the use of compasses or folding and cutting, as the shape will then lack interest and individuality. Most people who are already interested in textiles should not find this difficult as scissors will have already become an extension of the fingers. Working this way the results will be lively and personal.

Always be on the look out for possible shapes. In winter the shapes between the bare branches of trees are fascinating. Cut some of the shapes freely from your collection of coloured papers in a range of tones, perhaps varying the scale so that there will be some immediate contrasts. Shadows will yield good shapes, free from surface detail, so that attention can be focused on the shapes themselves. Reflections produce unusual shapes, too – those on shiny surfaces and those on water. Collect shells, leaves, stones and seedheads – in fact anything which suggests a starting point. Look at magazine illustrations upside down; there will be some surprises as you look at interesting shapes out of context. Other possibilities will suggest themselves, and the experience gained will lead to an increased perception of the value of **asymmetry**. This will not confine itself to embroidery, but will influence your judgement in other creative work.

You will find a small piece of **plaster board** useful for laying out proposed designs as the surface is soft enough to accept ordinary pins. Gather together your collection of coloured papers, shapes already cut out, a variety of yarns and scraps of felt and leather. Experiment with these on the board, moving the shapes around to try different placings. The emphasis may be horizontal or vertical; shapes may overlap or be placed at different levels. Pin satisfactory arrangements before bringing in the yarns and cords to create a linear interest.

Try out different types of line –
gently sinuous, coiling, sweeping
upwards – some lines may be
repeated to produce a sense of
rhythm as well as emphasis. Lines
may be continuous or broken and in
contrasting yarns. Some will break
the edges of shapes, others pass
underneath; all will add a textural
quality and produce changes of
colour and tone.

The intangible qualities of good
judgement in perception of shape,
line, colour, tone and texture do not
come as easily as learning stitches,
but when they do, it is deeply
satisfying.

*106 A patchwork cushion of plain and patterned squares is here joined
together in a chequer pattern. Some pattern squares have threads
withdrawn as in hardanger embroidery; others are worked in satin, rice
and rhodes stitches. The plain squares are in mosaic stitch using bottle
green wool.*

7 RUG CANVAS & LARGE SCALE WORK

Experimenting on canvas of various meshes, using as wide a variety of materials as possible, can be very stimulating. Before working on rug canvas it is necessary to overcast the edges. The canvas itself can be bought in different colours and sizes – an average size being three holes to the inch. Colours available are white, cream and natural. As we propose leaving some of the canvas threads unworked as part of the design, the colour can be quite important. Working on rug canvas extends the range of yarns and materials that can be used (*Fig. 107*). Rug and carpet wools and bunches of finer yarns are all suitable, along with strips of fabric, frayed on one or both edges. Velvet and knitting ribbons, braid, strips of leather, felt or strips of Vilene will add interesting contrasts. Try, also, piping cords, macramé twine and strips of nylon, cut spirally from stockings or tights (*Fig. 108*).

As mentioned before **leather strips** can be used to good effect in designing. These need to be cut accurately to fit into the selected canvas; the best way to achieve this is to cut the leather with a sharp knife and metal safety rule on a cutting tin. If this is not possible, then mark the cutting line on the wrong side of the leather and using sharp scissors cut with long smooth strokes. Strips about 1 cm (3/8 in.) wide can be used as a ribbon, passed vertically or horizontally under and over the threads of the canvas. Rather narrower strips of leather will look attractive when used as a fringe. Cut pieces twice the required finished length plus an

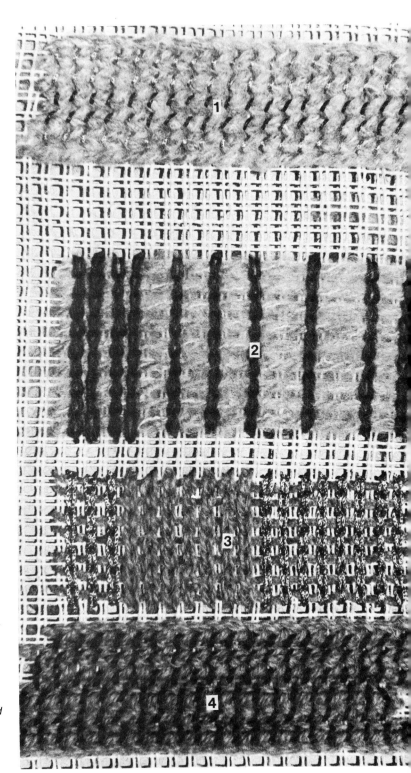

107 (1) Rows of chain stitch, made of fluffy knitting wool, worked horizontally over one thread of the canvas; the right hand side of the chain loop in one row is whipped to the left hand side of the loop in the next row, with a shiny rayon knitting yarn in shades of grey and tan.

(2) Chain stitch in spaced bands, worked in soft embroidery cotton threaded with fluffy knitting wool in silver grey.

(3) Chain stitch in spaced bands, worked in shiny knitting rayon and fluffy wool, threaded with orange chenille.

(4) A repeat of (1) above, using grey carpet wool and whipped with soft embroidery cotton.

108 (1) *Two bands of herringbone stitch, one using nylon stocking strips, the other rug wool in a contrasting colour. Cross stitches fill the space between the rows.*

(2) *Rows of chain stitch made of nylon stocking strips, the loops whipped together with a rug wool in contrasting colour.*

(3) *Rows of surrey stitch made of strips of nylon stocking and rug wool alternately. A centre band of laid rug wool is held down with cross stitches.*

(4) *Bands of stem stitch, four rows wide, with raised-chain band in rug wool between each group.*

(5) *Broad chain stitch made of nylon stocking strips and rug wool in a contrasting colour alternately.*

(6) *Surrey stitch made from nylon stocking strips in two different shades. All the loops are left uncut.*

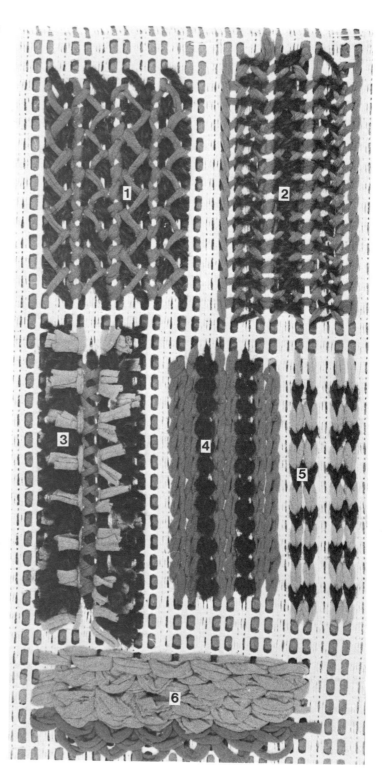

allowance to form the loop which should be inserted from the front, one canvas hole above the finishing line and emerge one hole below. Pull the two ends through the loop and arrange the head neatly. Repeat until the row is complete. It will add a strong contrast to other yarns and is texturally very exciting. Detached units of fringe of varying lengths can also be used, made both of leather and other materials.

Wider strips of fabric with frayed edges may be passed over two and under one thread of the canvas with

109 *(1) Two rows of back stitch worked with nylon stocking strips, threaded with contrasting rug wool. A central band of pekinese stitch also worked with nylon stocking strips and rug wool.*

(2) Rug wool laid in horizontal rows, varying in tone from top to bottom. Held down with button hole stitch in alternate holes, each row is encroaching. Button hole stitches also vary in colour from top to bottom.

(3) Strips of nylon stocking laid horizontally and vertically to form a grid, overlaid by another grid of rug wool. Cross stitches in a contrasting colour and thread worked over the intersections.

(4) Laid strips of nylon stocking forming a grid; each intersection is held down with tent stitch in perlé cotton.

(5) A grid of nylon stocking strips with upright cross stitches in rug wool over two horizontal and two vertical strips with alternate rows staggered.

(6) A variation of (5) with modified spacing.

(7) Strips of nylon stocking laid horizontally and vertically to form a grid. Alternate intersections tied down with cross stitches in rug wool, the other crossings with tent stitch in perlé cotton.

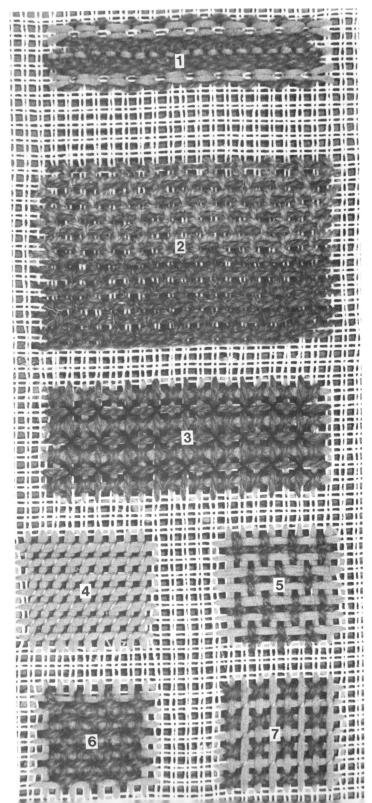

very pleasing textural results. The effect will vary according to the fabric used and the length of the fringed edges. If the rows are spaced apart, yarns or fine strips of felt can be added to develop a rich surface. **Nylon strips** used in the needle as the working thread need nothing to complement them as they look most attractive in the simplest of stitches (*Fig. 109*). The surface produced wears well so that it is particularly useful from a practical point of view besides being a contrasting material. Remember that the nylon strips can be dyed easily.

In addition to yarns, large beads, buttons – possibly wood – together with a bold use of bone, metal or plastic rings (*Fig. 110*) will make a lively impact. Sections of sawn-up bamboo can make an interesting contribution, particularly if used with a collection of other natural materials, such as raffia (*Fig. 111*) and cane. Work freely, trying out ideas and different combinations of materials.

110 *(1) Covered rings on a background of tent stitch. In the first, third and fifth blocks the rings are held down with straight stitches forming a star shape. The second and fourth blocks have two rings, one smaller than the other – the larger covered with lurex knitting yarn, the smaller with perlé cotton. They are tied down with straight stitches and with a bead in the centre.*

(2) Metal washers covered with lurex knitting yarn alternating with uncovered washers, overlapping and held in place by back stitches. One row of long legged cross stitch top and bottom.

(3) Uncovered washers arranged in a chequer pattern, held in place with four groups of three straight stitches. Finished with a central bead and with a row of three cross stitches in rug wool between each washer.

(4) Covered rings of different sizes attached to the canvas with cross stitches and lying on a band of trammed tent stitch in rug wool.

(5) Uncovered rings attached with two up-and-down buttonhole stitches, with one stitch between each pair. A cross stitch in a contrasting colour fills the centre.

(6) Uncovered rings are stitched down with a band of rice stitch in two contrasting shades of rug wool.

(7) Covered rings attached with straight stitches; sheaf filling stitch, worked between each pair of rings and the band completed with two rows of long-legged cross stitch.

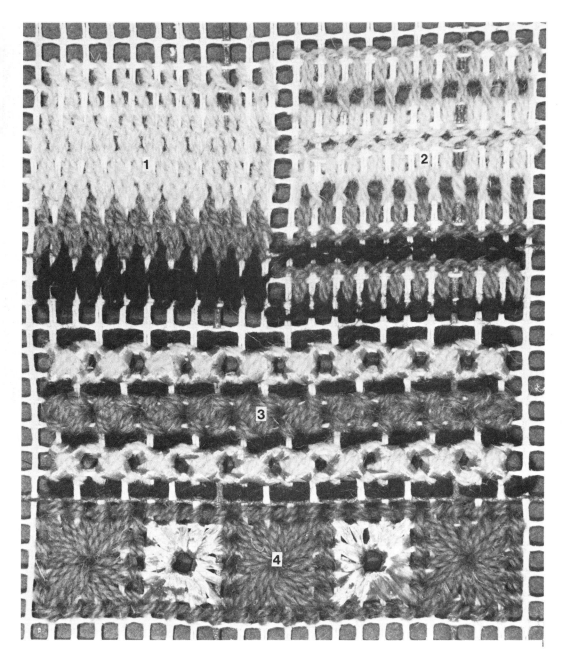

111 *(1) Cretan stitch in encroaching rows shading in colour from top to bottom.*

(2) Varied arrangements of up-and-down buttonhole stitch, the loops being threaded with rug wool in a contrasting colour.

(3) Three rows of rice stitch separated by one row of running stitches. Two of the rice stitch rows worked with a combination of rug wool and raffene.

(4) Eye stitches worked alternately in raffene, and rug wool is outlined with back stitches.

112 (1) Velvet fabric, cut into strips and darned through the mesh. Note the vertical stripes produced by the canvas threads. A row of double-cross stitch, is worked below.

(2) A strip of fabric passed vertically over three threads of the canvas.

(3) Brown carpet wool used to work diagonal detached chain stitches, separated by a row of stem stitch.

(4) An interesting natural wool mixture, used double, to work three rows of tent stitch.

(5) Three rows of encroaching knotted stitch, each passing over three canvas threads. Two rows, using rayon wool mixture double, and one, using rug wool.

(6) Detached chain stitches over one thread of canvas using a variegated rayon yarn in shades of gold, couch down gold carpet wool. Rows of stem stitch between, using the same yarns.

(7) Several strands in the needle give a different appearance from a single heavy yarn. Four strands of fine pink wool repeat **(3)** above.

(8) Two rows of running stitch followed by two of tent using natural rug wool. Note the prominent vertical bars of the canvas, which add to the pattern.

(9) A dark tone can be uninteresting if it is of uniform colour and texture. Here a square of dullish purple is made up of rows of stem stitch in purplish blue with a rayon yarn, followed by a row of double-cross stitch, using burgundy carpet wool. Two more rows of stem stitch in reddish purple are followed by double-cross stitch in purplish blue, stem stitch in burgundy, cross stitch in reddish purple and, finally, stem in purplish blue.

(10) Three rows of knotted stitch using double tapestry wool, in purple and scarlet. The rows do not encroach, thus leaving spaces which are filled with oblique detached chain stitches.

(11) Detached chain stitches worked diagonally in both directions using dish cloth cotton, enclosing a row in rust carpet wool and double perlé cotton. Stem stitch in pink and rust separates the bands.

(12) Four strands of carpet wool couched with double perlé cotton followed by four rows of tightly packed stem stitch, using brown carpet wool. One row of stem stitch using a rayon wool mix, in old gold, is followed by four more strands of carpet wool couched with perlé cotton. Detached diagonal chain stitches, stem stitch, couched

113 Floor cushion worked on rug canvas.

rug wool and knotted stitch in rows combine
to form a richly textured surface. As contrast,
a block worked by darning olive rayon yarn
over two threads and under one thread of the
canvas, followed by an alternating row, using
scarlet rayon. This textured block was the
basis of the design for the floor cushion in
Fig. 113.

(13) Double-cross stitch using old gold carpet
wool.

(14) As *(13)* above, but using dark brown
carpet wool combined with shiny gold rayon.

(15) Natural rug wool couched with perlé
cotton in light brown followed by double
cross stitch in natural and old gold carpet
wool. Running stitches separate the final
rows of cross stitch.

The idea of leaving threads of
canvas unworked to become part of
the pattern is still important. It was
appreciated, when working on rug
canvas, that the unworked bars did
contribute to the pattern quality,
because of the contrasting nature of
the material. On one sampler, a
particularly successful border
appeared containing unworked
white horizontal and vertical bars of
canvas, which made a striking
pattern against the scarlet and dark
olive of the Wilton carpet wools.
The most practical way to use it was
as the border of a floor cushion (*Fig.
113*) with the top surface completely
covered. Tied gobelin stitch in olive
was chosen for this. As the area was
large, about 45 cm square (18 in.),
the general effect, though practical,
could have looked uninteresting.
Eleven shades of olive and brown of
roughly equal tone were selected to
work the rows across. The result
was a blend which enhanced the
lively border. A sturdy olive rep was
used for the making up of the
underside of the cushion.

Complete coverage is required for
practical purposes where the
surface will be subject to heavy
wear, as in a floor cushion, stool or
chair seat. Probably the most useful
stitch for this, on rug canvas, is stem

114 *Chair.*

115 *Chair back.*

stitch, worked over the bars of the mesh using carpet wool. At least two rows should be worked in each space; the resulting surface is smooth. Back stitch, on the other hand, gives ribs which make an attractive textural contrast when used with the stem. Another stitch which covers well is tied gobelin; this is also texturally very attractive.

To use a fine yarn on rug canvas thread several strands in the needle. Experiments could be interesting as it would be a way of mixing colours or introducing a sheen to matt yarns.

The joy of making samplers comes from working enough of an idea to see its possibilities and being absolutely free from any kind of restraint. One idea nearly always leads to another or suggests the use of a different set of materials. *Colour plate 6* shows such a sampler, where making use of unworked threads in the mesh has, once again, made an attractive contribution to the design. In one example strips of navy

leather pass under and over the canvas leaving double white bars in sharp contrast. A fancy shiny rayon yarn in turquoise and green is worked in back stitch, resulting in shiny ribs. Stem stitch is then added, using carpet wools in different shades of turquoise, purple and rust.

Just at this time we were offered a tubular chair frame which needed a square piece of work for the seat and a rectangle for the back (*Figs 114 and 115*). One idea from the sampler was worked without any changes except that a 2 cm (¾ in.) border of stem stitch in dark turquoise was added. This produced the firm edge needed for making up and in use.

The depth of the border along the front edge was increased to 4 cm (1½ in.) to allow it to wrap round the bar.

Sometimes a small sample of a pattern may look attractive, but when repeated over a much larger area it loses its effectiveness. Laying on carpet wools horizontally in different colours showed that only a small addition was needed to enliven the design. Rust in two shades was selected and used to work horizontal bands on the two pieces; four bands were required on the seat and two on the back. Finally, each piece was lined with green upholstery linen which produced neatening and strengthening (*Fig. 115*). On rug canvas this project could obviously be carried out very rapidly and would enable people not able to manage fine embroidery to have the fun of using the colours and materials of their choice.

The two items just described were inspired by working samplers on rug canvas and experimenting with a variety of materials in a wide range of colours (*Fig. 116*). This underlines the need for working freely and trying out all the ideas that suggest themselves. Experiment also with stitches; since canvas can now be bought in a variety of mesh sizes all kinds of materials may now be used. *Colour plate 7* shows a sampler where interlaced herringbone has been worked in turquoise knitting ribbon. The stitches are five bars of canvas deep and four across. The second row in the same colour is attractively laced with the first. It would have been a mistake to use more than one colour as the pattern would tend to disintegrate. There should always be a good reason for changes in tone and colour.

Try other surface stitches, keeping the scale of materials in mind; some will accentuate the holes in the canvas.

Couching is a most useful and versatile stitch in large scale work and it can give a solidity to a design which may not be provided by some other stitches. Couching also has the virtue of allowing materials to be used which either do not pass through the canvas or are not shown to full advantage when broken up by canvas bars. Bunches of assorted yarns can be used like this, and the couching stitches should be considered as an important part of the appearance. Detached chain stitches are attractive, when used as the couching stitch, as they allow peeps of the couched material to show through the chain. The stitches may be worked vertically, horizontally or diagonally. All experiments should be looked at from different angles, upside down, sideways; they can suggest new starting points.

Interesting additions which might stimulate further ideas can come from other crafts such as macramé, knitting and crochet. Cords, strips and small shapes can be produced in a variety of yarns, laid on the canvas and built into a design with threads, so that the total effect may be envisaged and changed if necessary before you carry out any stitchery. **Plaiting** is attractive in its own right and can be incorporated as a braid. Single colours composed of different types of yarn can form the basis of a rich design. Metallic yarns may be included. Another way of using plaiting is to begin by wrapping the selected threads round two vertical threads of canvas and then plaiting. At any point the threads may be passed through to the back and emerge lower down. There could be many variations on this. The ends may be taken through

116 (1) Double stitch (oblong cross stitch over one horizontal and three vertical canvas threads, alternating with small cross stitches over one thread of canvas). Worked using rug wool in dark green and old gold.

(2) Four rows of running stitches over two threads of canvas, followed by a back stitch over one thread (back and running stitch). This is followed by up-and-down buttonhole stitch over different numbers of threads.

(3) Bands of long-legged cross stitch in shades of gold, separated by rows of blanket stitch in bottle green with a line of running stitches between each block.

(4) Two blocks of encroaching cretan stitch in graduated shades of old gold; the loops in the central band are linked with green raffene.

(5) A block of upright cross stitch in pale green, the spaces filled with tent stitch in dark green. Bands of satin stitch in dark green, top and bottom.

(6) Blocks of satin stitch in dark green and old gold with diagonal stitches filling the spaces.

(7) Blocks of three satin stitches worked into one hole of the canvas, the rows alternately light and dark green. Each dark green row has the stitch linking the blocks lying on the surface.

(8) A row of long-legged cross stitch, top and bottom, separated by trammed buttonhole stitch in encroaching rows. Bands top and bottom in dark green, the central band in graduated shades of gold.

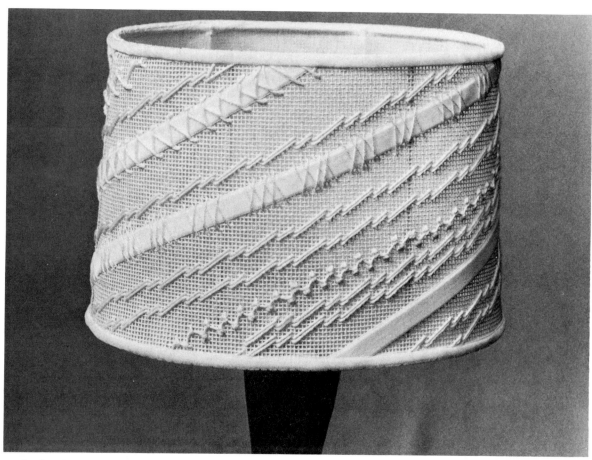

to the back and secured or knotted to produce a fringe which need not be uniform in length. Spaces between the plaits may be treated in a number of ways. Leather, felt or Vilene strips, threaded vertically under and over would contribute a flat quality, contrasting well with the textured plaiting. A good choice of stitches worked horizontally or vertically would add interest.

As an alternative to using rug canvas, large scale work may also be carried out on the coarser canvases. As canvas is naturally a stiffened material it is good for making lampshades. We show two examples made on canvas of 10 threads to the inch. The first, oval in

117 Lampshade designed and worked by Bridget Moss.

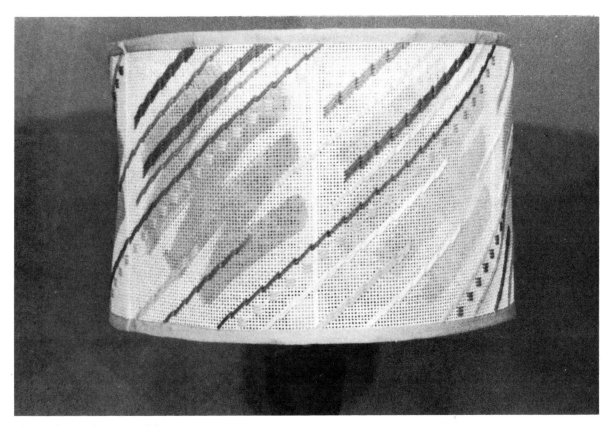

shape, is worked on white canvas
with white materials and is lined
with white muslin (*Fig. 117*). The
design is based on diagonal lines.
Three of these consist of white
velvet ribbon 1.5 cm wide (⅝ in.).
Two of the ribbons are held in place
by large stitches, the first with soft
cotton, the other No. 5 with perlé
cotton; one of the ribbons is left
plain, in contrast. Between these
bands are diagonal rows of knotted
herringbone and diagonal straight
stitches in pairs, alternately long
and short, worked in soft cotton.
Because the canvas is taut and the
yarn substantial, all the work
appears raised from the surface,
giving rich textures which are most
attractive. The shade is finished at
the top and bottom edges with
folded velvet ribbon.

118 Lampshade designed and worked by Bridget Moss.

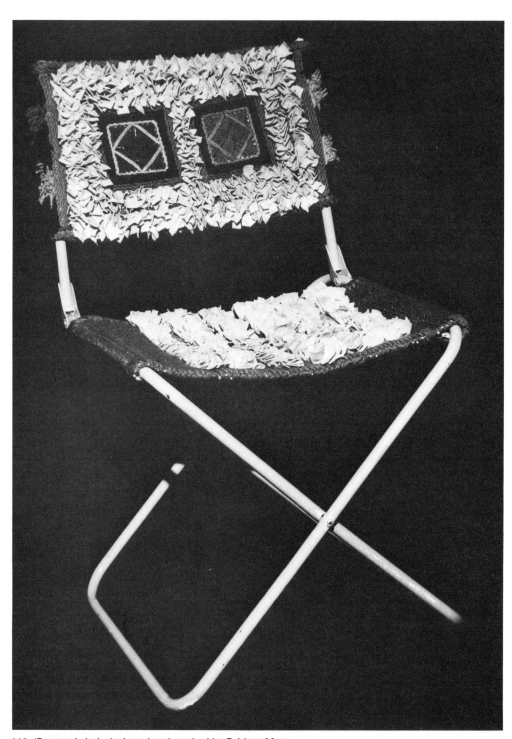

119 'Rag-rug' chair designed and worked by Bridget Moss.

120 *Chair back.*

The second shade is round and much larger in size, 35 cm across (14 in.) (*Fig. 118*). The special feature here is the use of oil paint to create brightly coloured brush strokes as a basis for the stitches. It is essential to use materials for this which do not make the canvas limp, as water-based dyes would. The work must be left for at least a week to allow the surface to become completely dry. The free diagonal strokes are in bright pink and orange which look well on the cream canvas. Yarns in soft cotton include yellow, orange, scarlet, magenta, purple pink and lime green. The stitches used are diagonal straight stitches in pairs and sometimes in fours which touch. Other horizontal straight stitches in groups of three form small squares. A few of the original brush strokes remain unworked. For the rest, diagonal lines stream up along edges or through the middle of the broad strokes. There are also lines of stitching starting or finishing on the unpainted canvas. Everything takes the same diagonal direction and there is a terrific sense of vitality. Straight cotton binding, which picks up the pinky-orange colour of one of the oil paints, completes the design, top and bottom.

If familiar with the rag rug technique you will be interested in the small tubular frame folding chair (*Fig. 119*). Stockinet in grey and peach is used for the tufting. Pieces are cut on the straight, approximately 5 cm x 2 cm (2 in. x ¾ in.). You will need two pieces of worked canvas for the seat and for the back. Cut rug canvas, three holes to the inch, with ample turnings both for neatening and for wrapping round the chair frame.

Work the background of the seat in stem stitch, using two strands of mid-rust rug wool, the rows running from front to back. There is a central square area of tufting. Three rows of grey alternate with three rows of peach, separated by rows of stem stitch worked in wool ranging in colour from light to dark rust, six rows of each. Front and back edges of the canvas are folded under and a plaited edge stitch worked through both thicknesses in matching rust wool.

For the back, work a large rectangle, taking up nearly all the area, in two rows of peach tufting (*Fig. 120*). The area inside is broken into two squares, outlined by two rows of grey tufting. Work two smaller inside squares with wools in four shades of rust, using stem stitch, herringbone and straight stitch. Sufficient rows of mid-rust must be worked at each end to curve round the frame and, on the extreme ends,

make fringes using all the shades of rust. Line the back with grey cotton.

A small panel, *Waterfall* (*Colour plate 8*), worked on cream canvas with 10 threads to the inch, uses a variety of materials, all within a narrow range of natural colours, dominated by unspun sheep's fleece in shades of grey, dark brown and natural. Hand-spun Jacob's fleece in shades of light grey to almost black is also used. All this wool is the perfect foil for the sparkle to be introduced in the form of black and silver yarn and white Lystwist, a yarn of high sheen. Silver leather, cut into narrow strips also makes a significant contribution. These are placed against the dark band of stitches, half way down, and are secured only at the ends, so that they stand away and catch the light. Half way down the same band are long white Lystwist tassels, some of which are mixed with the black and silver yarns. These fall right to the base and a few, longer than the rest, help to create a tapering overall shape. The band below is in mid-grey hand-spun, slightly longer than the previous band, but not as wide. Finally, at the base, is a mixture of lightly spun wool from natural to almost black. Here the stitches are longer still and of varying lengths with the longest placed towards the centre. In all three bands the stitch used is part-rhodes. Two rows of full-rhodes stitch are worked in hand spun, which in their solidity contrast with the flowing effect below. The top five rows are more tightly organised in contrast. The dominant row of brown fleece is couched in Lystwist, the other one likewise, but with closer white stitching and, immediately below, there is a compact group of twinkling black and silver, followed by two further rows. Free fleece hangs at the sides.

We have been looking at a wide range of materials that can be happily used on rug canvas. *Fig. 121* shows a very exciting piece which uses strips cut from a beautiful fabric from Bernat Klein, renowned for his rich colours. Dark sage green and muted turquoise are the only plain colours; with multicolours including various greens, blues and turquoise. Some of the mixtures include white and also pale shades of the stronger colours. The strips of fabric are cut on the straight about 2.5 cm (1 in.) wide and are used together with knitting ribbon in pale mauvish blue and bright clear turquoise. The ribbon not only gives a finer line but, because of the change in the nature of the fabric, plays an important part in producing gentle emphasis to the diagonal basis of the design. The stitches used are stem and back stitch. The darning stitches worked with fabric strips pass over three threads of canvas, both vertically and horizontally. As the stitches are spaced on the diagonal, all the holes are filled and the canvas completely covered. Back stitch is used as a line and also as a filling in 3 cm (1¼ in.) bands. It passes diagonally over the intersections of the canvas threads.

The worked piece measures 38 x 64 cm (15 x 25 in.). The design is simple, roughly diagonally symmetrical. There is a 5 cm (2 in.) wide rich band of deep blue and turquoise across the centre. It is flanked on either side by bands about 2.5 cm (1 in.) wide in mid-turquoise, followed by others in very pale shades. The sharp change in tones produces an interesting central band, measuring 18 cm (7 in.) across. This is further increased by varied 2.5 cm bands, including two where strips have been used to work back stitch. This enlarged area measures 40 cm

121 *Panel designed and worked by Bridget Moss.*

(16 in.) across. The two remaining triangles, 16 cm (6½ in.) deep, are worked in sage green with bright turquoise and pale mauve knitting ribbon lines in stem. Other lines in back stitch are worked in multi-coloured strips. The total effect is stimulating.

8 DEVELOPMENT

Some of the finished items shown in this chapter are the outcome of the experiments carried out on samplers worked before any of the objects were considered. The exciting and unforseen results sometimes prompted the later working and making up of an item, although this was definitely not the primary objective. Two such objects were described in the last chapter: the floor cushion and the tubular chair.

On another sampler, illustrated in the chapter on materials (*Fig. 4*), purple velvet ribbon, black chenille, and black and silver yarn combine to form a rich border. Two pieces of purple velvet ribbon are stitched down with up-and-down buttonhole stitch, one using saxe blue and the other black and silver yarn. The two strips of ribbon are spaced to allow three black chenille threads to be couched in up-and-down button hole stitch using black and silver yarn; all stitches alternate. This small sampler suggested the design on the jewellery box shown in *Fig. 122*. A purple cotton fabric, used in the making up, contrasts with the rich texture of the stitches. Two further box designs in the form of buildings with removable roofs are seen in *Figs 123 and 124*.

122 Jewellery box.

123 Model of a thatched cottage. The chequer pattern for the upper storey has alternate dark and light pairs of cashmere stitch. Roof of laid stitches edged with velvet stitch. Fine details to door and windows are done in tent stitch.

124 Model of a shop using straight gobelin stitch for the roof in shades of purple and maroon. Walls in weaving yarn are held by close couching stitches in shades of red. Corners in mosaic stitch squares are put against a background of tent stitch. Items in the windows are worked in tent stitch and then covered with grey chiffon, which is held in place by the black tent stitches which outline the frames.

125 *Handbag with black leather handles.*

In a second experimental piece, illustrated in the chapter on texture, strips of coral felt and suede leather were used and alternated with double threads of claret chenille. Up-and-down button hole stitches in black wool and black and silver yarn were worked in groups. This design was incorporated in a handbag (*Fig. 125*). A variety of yarns were used: black and silver yarn, stranded and perlé cotton and some coloured threads in shades of claret. All stitches were worked with the knotted edge uppermost. Black leather handles completed the bag.

In *Fig. 98* (p. 81) there is a different type of sampler worked on yellow canvas and based on blackwork counted thread stitches. One of the patterns consisted of black triangles with triangles of unworked canvas

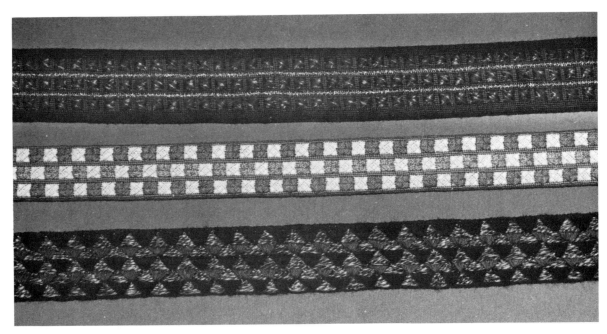

between each. From this simple basis an attractive necklace was designed. *(Colour plate 10.)* Seven wedges of canvas, 5 cm (2 in.) wide at the top and 7.5 cm (3 in.) at the base and 14 cm (5½ in.) deep, were covered with black organdie. The mesh shows through clearly. Triangles in yellow, old gold and sage green together with gold and silver lurex were worked in groups. Between each pair of wedges hang long tassels in matching yarns. Loops on the outside edges of the first and last wedge hold a hand-made cord, finished with similar tassels.

It was surprising to see how the stitches in macramé twine stood away from the canvas, producing a sculpted-look, seen in the sampler on p. 24 *(Fig. 21).* A soft embroidery cotton in a darker tone was added, but it may be possible to find twines in darker shades. When spring stitch is worked, interesting areas of canvas are left between the stitches. At the bottom of the sampler, where

126
Three belts:
(1) Five rows of milanese stitch, worked in contrasting tones of turquoise and bottle green, are repeated along the length of the belt, which is lined with bottle green cotton.

(2) Three bands of interlaced cross stitch, separated by lines of tent stitch. In rows one and three, macramé twine and soft embroidery cotton are used for alternate squares. In the centre band macramé twine alternates with perlé cotton.

(3) Three bands of rhodes stitch are separated by rows of tent stitch, using a lurex knitting yarn. Each cushion square is separated by vertical blocks of tent stitch.

wheat-sheaf stitch has been worked, vertical threads of canvas have been left exposed as part of the pattern.

Macramé twine has been used in other articles. It makes a distinctive feature, contrasting with wool on the folding chair.

A belt designed with three rows of squares separated by two rows of tent stitch (*Fig. 126*) used macramé twine alternating with gold perlé cotton in the centre row and with soft fawn, top and bottom. The squares were worked in interlaced cross stitch.

Another article using macramé twine was a shoulder bag, measuring about 40 cm x 30 cm (16 in. x 12 in.) (*Fig. 127*). Slate blue, rust and dark fawn soft cotton combined with the twine. Each side of the bag was planned with three wide vertical bands, separated by two narrow ones. Worked in twine using double-tied oblong cross stitch, this gives a pleasant textural quality; the source of this design can be seen in the macramé sampler in *Fig. 21*.

Some interesting experiments using narrow satin ribbon, about 3 mm wide (⅛ in.), combined with wool and perlé cotton, produced rich surfaces. Two samplers of open laid fillings are shown in *Fig. 74* and *Colour plate 1*. Another experiment used the ribbons threaded in the needle to work coral knot stitch. The ribbons can be held in place using cretan stitch and cross stitch or used to thread through vertical bars of an open laid filling. Another example shows a twill weave, produced by laying vertical threads in wool and threading with ribbon.

From these examples a design for a belt developed (*Fig. 128*). A few

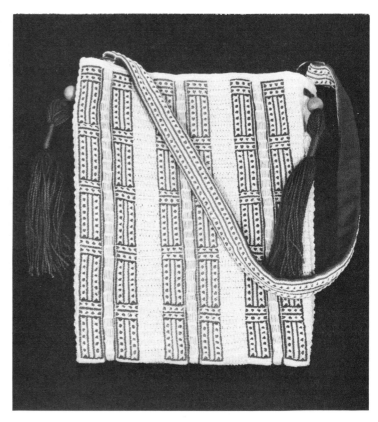

127 Shoulder bag made from macramé twine.

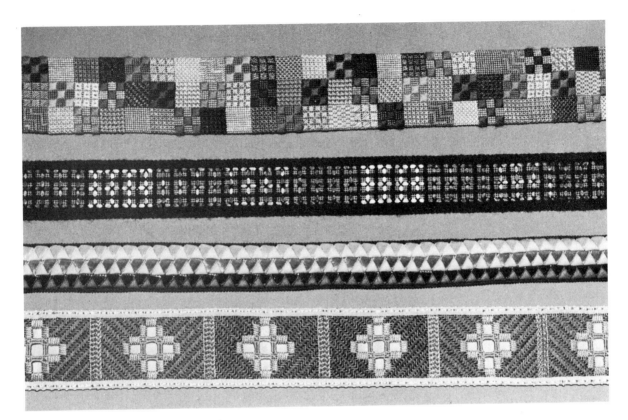

modifications were necessary: the spacing of the ribbon was changed to allow squares of unworked canvas to form part of the pattern and wool of the same colour was used throughout, so that the shapes were emphasized. The belt has blocks of pink, purple and emerald ribbons repeated along its length, the intersections being held in place by cross stitches in shiny black rayon. The edges are folded over and plait stitch in black wool worked through two thicknesses of canvas. The lining is of black cotton.

Velvet ribbon in various widths and colours has been introduced in several samplers. The pile surface makes an interesting contrast with the back of the ribbon, and this feature has been exploited by folding in different ways. A belt

128
Four belts:

(1) Shades of pink using a variety of stitches which include mosaic, cross, tent and eyelets, but some uniformity is kept by repetition of the square shapes.

(2) Narrow ribbon laid in a mesh pattern, held down by cross stitches in black knitting cotton. This belt is described fully in this chapter.

(3) Folded velvet ribbon in beige, pale green and bottle green, folded to expose the underside. Based on an idea shown in Fig. 74.

(4) Pattern darning in shades of mauve and purple as a background to kloster blocks as used in hardanger embroidery; the background changes colour along the length.

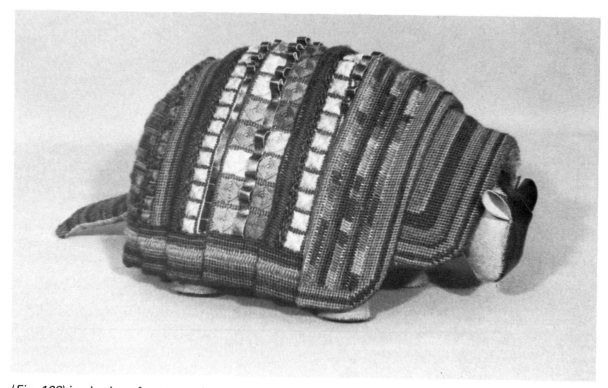

129 Armadillo.

(Fig. 128) in shades of green and stone uses three rows of folded ribbon, arranged so that triangles are formed. Each fold is held in place by a horizontal straight stitch which is concealed by the next fold. The technique is similar to the one used when gold plate is applied in ecclesiastical embroidery.

All these articles evolved from experiments on canvas; sometimes, however, the decision to make a specific object comes first, and experimental samplers are worked with this article in mind. A terracotta armadillo from Columbia had always been a favourite and prompted the making of another in embroidery. Canvas was the ideal material to use because of its stiffness (Fig. 129). Lampshade wire was formed into the basic shape for the shell. The body was created from felt in the way that soft toy animals are made. Tapestry wools

in shades of purple, old gold, olive and pink were matched in soft cotton with the addition of scarlet. Mauve felt, for making the body, matched the colour of one of the wools but, after making up, was not much in evidence (*Fig. 130*).

At an early stage in the experiments it was decided that copper-coloured leather should be added for the head as a shiny contrast, with similar strips across the back to enrich the worked bands. Some of the strips were manipulated into humps to give texture. The shell of the animal was built up from overlapping segments, the shapes of which were derived from paper patterns, starting from the tail and moving along to the head.

At this point the sample pieces in the chapter on texture (*Fig. 70*) on p. 55 were worked to see how colours and stitches would combine. Each piece began and

130 *Underside of armadillo, showing construction.*

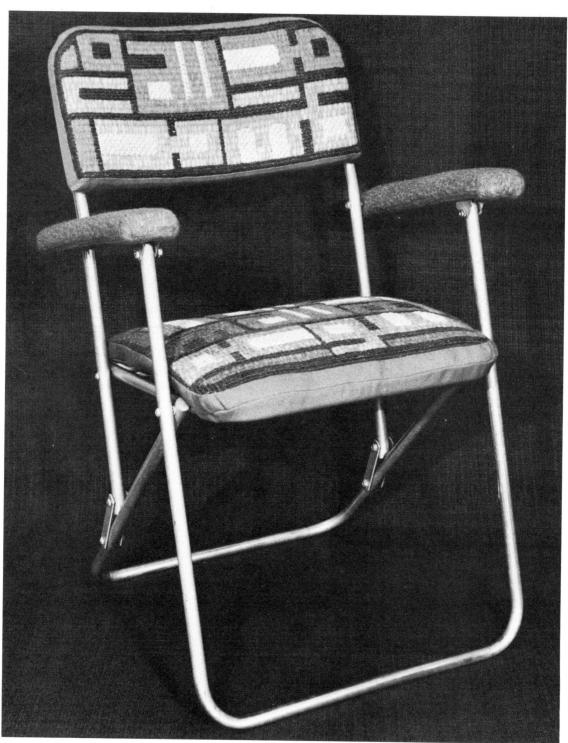

131 Folding chair.

132 *Back panel of folding chair.*

ended with a simple border in tent stitch, enclosing a richly developed central band. White was included in the experiments but it soon became clear that this detracted from the rich effect. Norwich stitches proved successful but the idea of leather squares was dropped as they broke up the effect of the central band. Change of colour in two of the norwich stitches was also a mistake and was abandoned. Although the worked experiments were helpful, it was essential that we kept ideas flexible and made continuous judgements, looking for contrasts in colour, tone and texture.

The next object for which no sampler yet existed was a folding chair (*Fig. 131*). A tubular framed chair with arms and padded seat was available, presenting new problems. We cut paper patterns to determine the shapes required for the back, seat and tapering arm pieces. These shapes were marked out on to the canvas with a generous turning allowance. A new sampler

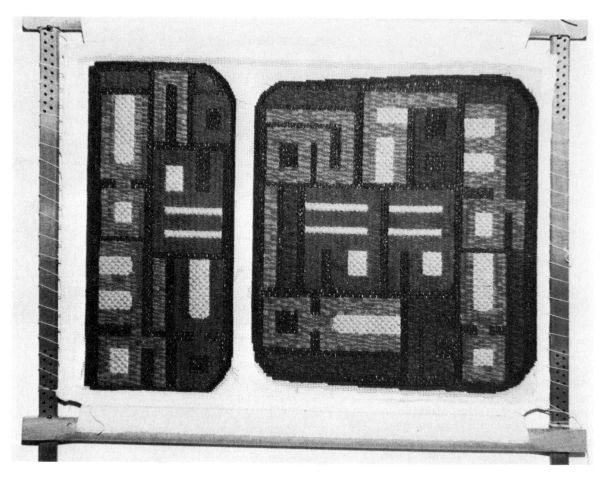

133 *Worked panels for folding chair mounted on embroidery frame.*

was worked using carpet wools in rust, bottle green, black, brown and grey with scraps of macramé twine tentatively included (*Fig. 97*). Suitable stitches for close coverage included stem stitch, worked horizontally in a mixture of yarns and tied gobelin in a mixture of bottle green and rust using matt and shiny yarns. Other experiments included encroaching single chains, half-drop part-rhodes, tent and gobelin mixed and blocks of surrey stitch.

Ideas for the design developed at a time when there was a national interest in Islamic traditional patterns. Simple shapes, using mainly straight lines, were cut out and arranged on the paper patterns made for the seat and back. These shapes were then used as templates for transferring to the canvas. For the background two colour mixtures were used, a light mixture of orange and rust and a darker one of scarlet and brown (*Fig. 132*). Colours allowed to mix in the eye are always more interesting than a single shade. Strong dark tones of brown and bottle green emphasized the linear shapes, with the main shapes in two shades of rust. There remained some small unworked areas within these larger shapes which were filled with part-rhodes stitch, worked in natural macramé twine. Khaki rep was used in the making up.

Small pieces of canvas used for experiments can be held in the hand for working but larger pieces, such as those for the chair, need to be mounted in an embroidery frame as seen in *Fig. 133* which shows the main components of one of the chairs. After completion, the work should be damp stretched – that is, laid on wet blotting paper or sheeting, stretched, pinned out on a board so that the threads lie correctly and allowed to dry. When completely dry it is ready for making up.

A house brick was the basis of a door stop (*Fig. 134*). Pieces cut from an old blanket provided padding all round, with extra layers on top. Five pieces of canvas were required, the base being finished with felt in a matching colour. The design needed to be simple, depending on good colour and contrasting tone. Measurements were taken after padding, allowing generous turnings, and transferred to paper patterns on which the design was worked out. Shapes may be cut in paper and laid on the prepared pieces. The door stop has the design unit repeated three times across the top, with one unit at each end. Bands suggesting a repetition of the unit continue over the sides. Long back stitches, worked in dark green and brown carpet wool, outline all the units, with additional bands of stem and tent stitches in bright orange, tan, scarlet and magenta. The old gold background is made up of alternate rows of gobelin and tent stitch.

Three of the small bins which are illustrated were made for use in children's rooms. They can be used as storage for small objects and add colour and interest to the room. Round tins are readily available in various sizes. Accurate measurements with generous seam allowances are essential. The area available for the design is marked out on paper, and the main shapes cut out; try out various placings in the space until a satisfactory arrangement is obtained. The shapes should be as large as can easily be accommodated within the area and so arranged that the design is satisfactory at the point where the join is made. By experimenting with the arrangement of the design elements it is possible to avoid the seam cutting through a main motif. The shapes are used as templates to transfer the design to the canvas.

In previous chapters we have emphasized the importance of filing every worked experiment for future reference. Although no sampler was worked specifically for these bins there was a fund of design ideas to draw upon.

The first two examples use animals as their main theme (*Colour plate 11*), and the finished articles are quite small, about 17 cm. (6½ in.) tall and of similar diameter.

On the tiger bin, the two beasts curve round the bin, their tails forming useful design links. The bodies have black stripes against a broken coloured background which includes orange, tan, and greenish gold. The heads in tent stitch are mainly white with the features in honey coloured leather and black stitchery. Blanket stitch in coton à broder makes a broken edge round the heads. The background, worked in tent stitch, is shaded from top to bottom, starting with pale turquoise, gradually introducing emerald green, replacing the turquoise with jade green and, at the base, the darkest shade of green. The top edge of the bin is finished with a band of dark green tent stitch and has a golden brown felt lining.

The tigers have a companion on the lion bin. The lion's head is in shades of golden brown against a purple background. Tent stitch in two tones of brown is used for the face, the eyes being made of black leather outlined in yellow; the nose, a piece of padded suede and the muzzle in white tied gobelin stitch. (Do not use beads when making toys or other objects for children.)

Whiskers are loosely stitched in fine white perlé cotton. For the mane, pekinese stitch worked vertically in a variety of yarns and colours produces a good contrast to the flat tent stitch area. The inclusion of white for muzzle, ears, whiskers and mane is an important design detail. The purple background needed to be interesting, though was of secondary importance. Irregular blocks and stripes in gobelin, cross and tent stitches, using purple and purplish blue give areas of textural interest as a foil to the stitchery on the head. The edge of the bin is finished off with a band of tent stitch and lined with purple felt.

134 *Door stop using a house brick.*

135 *The clown bin.*

Quite a different theme is used on the third bin (*Fig. 135*). This is taller, 20 cm (8 in.), and wider which allows space for three clowns. The design was developed using cut paper, as described previously. The best way to obtain lively movement is to cut the head, body, arms and legs separately and move them, relative to one another, until the required effect is produced. Balls, hoops and balloons form links between the figures. Hot colours were chosen to work the clowns against a striped background of emerald and dark blue. Sharp contrast comes from the use of white for face and hands. Some leather was introduced for the features and a shiny yarn glints among the wool. An irregular arrangement of the striped background in gobelin and tent stitch adds interest. A band of tent stitch finishes the top, with a greenish yellow lining in felt and a dark blue

136 Bins based on geometric designs. Bin on the left designed and worked by Gisela Banbury.

cotton base. The small patterns used on the figures had been developed on earlier samplers.

The two remaining bins in *Fig. 136* are of more general use and could be used elsewhere in the house.

The bin on the left has a simple geometric design, which is carried out in tent stitch. The shapes worked with wool in coral, black and pink, stand out in relief against the light coloured areas, which are in stranded cotton. Other areas are emphasized by the application of padded, dark coloured shapes, made by covering card with fine cotton. Finished at the top with four rows of tent stitch in the colours already used, the bin is lined with cream coloured cotton.

The taller bin, on the right, has two bands of modified florentine stitch, worked horizontally in alternate groups of gold and maroon. Across the centre of the shaded gold shape are two rhodes stitches outlined with tent stitch. Worked in a shiny linen thread in shades of pink and maroon this contrasts well with the matt surface of the wool. The lower band is wider, the two being separated by a border of two rhodes stitches in burgundy, followed by three groups of horizontal satin stitch in tan. Finished off top and bottom with vertical rows of satin stitch in burgundy, it is lined with tan cotton.

Included amongst the illustrations are a group of panels. The first takes as its theme an onion which can be developed in different ways. In one (*Fig. 137*), a large piece of natural linen covers two thirds of the background. The onion shape covers the join between canvas and linen, with some of the stitchery worked through both. Areas of linen have been cut away to expose the

white canvas. Pairs of satin stitches add textural interest and emphasize the onion shape. No bright colours have been used; everything is in shades of white, cream and fawn, providing an unusual foil for the couched gold thread and the central padded shape of gold orion cloth. The onion and its leaves are worked entirely in stem stitch, variety being achieved by changing the weight of yarns used. Couching in white, gold and cream, outlines the linen shapes at the base and the padded orion cloth shape is overworked in spaced button hole stitch, varying in tone from light to dark.

A completely different treatment of the key elements of the onion design is shown in *Fig. 138*.

Spring Hat (*Fig. 139*) shows the free use of materials. Narrow satin ribbon in cream and pale blue makes loops; circles of plain and patterned transparent materials are stitched in the centre with a single stitch, to look like flowers; and suffolk puffs introduce larger shapes. White rayon cords, perlé cotton, Bernat Klein wools and an assortment of fancy yarns are used freely in the remaining spaces. The brim is worked in a flat darning stitch and edged with a single row of cream ric-rac braid. The face in cream cotton is of secondary importance.

The third panel is titled *Spring Cabbage* (*Colour plate 12*), showing design possibilities in the most unlikely subject. Worked on cream canvas, the applied shapes for the outer leaves are of plain and corded velvet in shades of green. Three of these shapes show the exposed canvas where the velvet has been cut away. As contrast, smaller areas of wool tufting, in shades of pink, draw the eye to the centre and

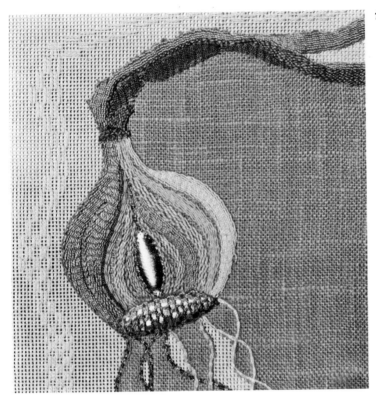

137 Panel based on onion motif.

138 A second treatment of the onion motif.

139 Panel, 'Spring Hat'.

across to another area of tufting in shades of green, gold and lemon. The remaining spaces are worked in rice, cross and tent stitches using pink and olive green wool and multicoloured perlé cotton. In the heart of the cabbage there is a tiny area of strong pink and magenta in tent stitch using a shiny yarn, surmounted by one large rhodes stitch. A mixture of green and yellow cross stitches lead to an exciting group of squares built up of diagonal stitches in lemon, lime, green and gold, with one thread of canvas left unworked between each square. Cuts in the canvas allow velvet ribbons in fawn and green to be threaded behind the worked squares. The total effect is a lively chequer pattern. With such a strong design an enriched background was required, and this was produced with pairs of horizontal stitches in heavy shiny rayon.

These three designs illustrate the unlimited scope for the development of creative ideas. They show the importance of proportion, texture and colour and the use of interesting materials.

The detailed descriptions read in conjunction with the preceding chapters will, we hope, give a clear idea of the process of designing. Emphasis has been given to the importance of a large selection of experimental samplers for use as starting points. A flexible approach is necessary, and a willingness to abandon any idea, no matter how precious, which does not contribute to the required effect. Designs need not be determined by the rigid horizontals and verticals of the canvas weave, nor need tapestry and crewel wools be the only threads used. We hope that we have shown that the freedom that has developed in other embroidery techniques is equally possible when working on canvas.

BIBLIOGRAPHY

Barker, J. *Making plaits and braids*. Batsford, London, 1973
Beaney, J. *Embroidery, new approaches*. Pelham Books, 1980
Beaney, J. *Textures and surface patterns*. Pelham Books, 1978
Butler, A. and Green, D. *Pattern and embroidery*. Batsford, London 1970.
Heartung, R. *Creative textile craft*. Batsford, London, 1964
Howard, C. *Inspiration for embroidery*. Batsford, London, 1966
Howard, C. *Book of stitches*. Batsford, London, 1979
Howard, C. *Embroidery and colour*. Batsford, London, 1976
Liley, A. *Embroidery*. A fresh approach. Mills and Boon, 1964
Morris, M. *Creative thread design*. Batsford, London, 1974
Nordfors, J. *Needle lace and needle weaving*. Studio Vista, 1974
Krevitsky, N. *Stitchery art and craft*. Van Nostrand Reinhold, 1974
Rhodes, M. *A dictionary of canvas work stitches*. Batsford, London, 1980
Risley, C. *Creative embroidery*. Studio Vista, 1969
Seyd, M. *Designing with string*. Batsford, London, 1967
Short, E. *Introducing macramé*. Batsford, London, 1970
Springall, D. *Canvas embroidery*. Batsford, London, 1980
Thomas, M. *A dictionary of embroidery stitches*. Hodder and Stoughton, London, 1934
Whyte, K. *Design in embroidery*. Batsford, London, 1982

INDEX

INDEX OF STITCHES

Italic numbers indicate pages on which stitch diagrams appear.